"We white Christians engage in conversation about a number of important issues. But there is one conversation we are loathe to have: talk about race. We get edgy and nervous when talk turns to 'America's original sin.' Carolyn Helsel gives us the background, the context, and the history we need in order to engage in this painful but so very important conversation. Helsel also gives us specific, practical guidance in how to instigate conversations about race in our churches. Thanks to God for this useful, important book!"

— Will Willimon, Duke Divinity School, United Methodist bishop, retired, and author of *Who Lynched Willie Earle?: Preaching to Confront Racism*

"Helsel wades right into the thicket of emotions that accompany white fragility. This book is a tender journey through the forest of avoidance, defensiveness, and obliviousness and a tool for building one's tolerance for truth. She pierces myths that undergird white supremacy and offers preachers and teachers a resource for sparking some conversations that desperately need to start. This volume is packed with stories that need to be heard if America is ever going to live out a new story concerning race."

— Donyelle McCray, Yale Divinity School

"'I'm not a racist,' you may be thinking. 'I'm not in the KKK and I don't carry a Nazi flag. Why should I read a book about race?' Carolyn Helsel's new book will answer that question, and in the process, you'll become ... not just a better white person, but a better, more mature, more caring Christian and human being."

— Brian D. McLaren, author of *The Great Spiritual Migration*

"This book is spot-on for the kinds of conversations we need to be having. Carolyn Helsel offers ready access to approach the hard issues of race without being adversarial. Her writing is deeply personal, reflecting her own path of growth. At the same time it is acutely informed by developmental theory and is pervaded by a generous pastoral sensibility."

> — Walter Brueggemann, Columbia Theological Seminary,
> author of *Sabbath As Resistance, The Prophetic Imagination*

"The author has engaged a critical step in dismantling racism: moving beyond the anxiety and hesitancy that many whites have about discussing the subject. Hard conversations must be had, and this book will be an important tool in facilitating them. The reader will be grateful for Carolyn's honest courage."

> — Teresa Hord Owens, General Minister and President,
> Christian Church (Disciples of Christ) in the United States
> and Canada

"*Anxious to Talk about It* builds a bridge for white Christians who don't want to be racist, but who don't have the tools or language to build an anti-racist identity. Rooted in both a Christian religious practice as well as a rigorous commitment to racial justice, Helsel addresses common barriers to racial awareness, including colorblindness, guilt, and resentment about PC culture. Direct, clear, and replete with illustrative stories, the book offers both invitation and inspiration to white Christians to grow and change in liberatory anti-racist ways, as well as the tools to do so."

> — Ali Michael, author of *Raising Race Questions: Whiteness,*
> *Inquiry and Education*

"*Anxious to Talk about It* is rooted in scholarly knowledge that branches into pastoral wisdom. White people usually do not want to talk about race, and when they do, often discover that they do not know how. Helsel takes seriously white anxiety about racism and provides keys to understanding the cultural, personal, and spiritual issues that it entails. This book is full of faith, and gives people of faith an accessible strategy to move beyond anxiety and guilt toward grace and gratitude. This is a book to be used, not just read."

> — Daniel Aleshire, retired Executive Director, The Association of Theological Schools in the United States and Canada

"Carolyn B. Helsel has placed her finger on a most anxious place in our society: racism and the awkward silence on this issue in many pulpits. With a scholar's insight and a pastor's wisdom, she provides counsel about how preachers in white contexts can speak about race with courage, thoughtfulness, and practical impact. This is an urgent, timely, and welcome book."

> — Thomas G. Long, Candler School of Theology

"From guilt and shame to healthy white identity, Helsel has brought us a much-needed guide to white self-awareness on the switchback-ridden journey to becoming anti-racist."

> — Sharon E. Watkins, Director, National Council of Churches Truth and Racial Justice Initiative

"'Anxious' is a much-needed resource to demystify the 'R' word (racism) for white people. This book is an inviting and accessible read for individuals and small groups. Helsel adeptly employs the art of storytelling to disarm those plagued by feelings of anger, confusion, and guilt when participating in anti-racism discussions. She impressively escorts the reader through an introduction to critical race theory as an invitation to help participants embrace their discomfort and own their 'response-ability' toward becoming an ally in the movement for racial justice."

> — April G. Johnson, Minister of Reconciliation, Christian Church (Disciples of Christ)

"In *Anxious to Talk About It,* a welter of stories that are real and get real invite 'white Christians' to recognize and relinquish racist ways, however subconscious, subtle, or insidious. Using narrative finesse, Helsel gently convicts readers to rely upon gratitude for the grace of God as an entrée into 'response-able listening' that fearlessly and attentively loves all neighbors, especially ones devastated by the sin of white racism. Churches and communities beyond her targeted audience will also feel the warmth and promise of her witness."

— Gerald C. Liu, Princeton Theological Seminary, author of *Music and the Generosity of God*

"Carolyn Helsel's book is 'for such a time as this.' It is an honest, courageous, thoughtful, and pastoral approach in engaging whites who are anxious to talk about race and racism. Helsel is brave enough to speak truth to power in these anxious and angry times. Reading this should move one prayerfully from anxiety to gratitude because the truth dances all over these pages. Beware (white) readers: you will meet the truth and the truth will set you free! If you dare to be free, 'take up and read.'"

— Luke A. Powery, Dean, Duke University Chapel

"Carolyn Helsel's book is full of stories, including moving stories about her own attempts to understand the power of racism and the need for faithful action to resist it. But she does not pretend to be perfect. She does not claim to have it all figured out. Her modesty opens up space for some frank conversations about race. And these are conversations that the church very much needs to be having."

— Ted A. Smith Candler School of Theology

What if I say the wrong thing? Is race really something that I need to talk about (I'm white)? Shouldn't I let people of color be the ones to bring it up? I don't want to offend anyone. I don't think I'm racist, but what if I say something that sounds racist? It's on the news all the time, but I don't know how to talk about what's going on. I'm worried someone will call me a racist. I don't see color. Why do we have to keep talking about this? I feel stupid when we talk about race. I realize there's a lot I don't know. But it's not my fault! I am not a racist. I work with people of color and I'm respectful and friendly to them like I treat anybody else. I have friends who are people of color and who don't want to talk about race, so why should we? I get angry thinking you're trying to make me more politically correct. Leave me alone already. What does this have to do with faith? The Bible doesn't say anything about race. Let's leave it alone. But what I saw happening on the news...some people are crazy and racist. But that's not me. But how do I stop something like that happening in my town? I don't know. It makes me anxious.

ANXIOUS TO TALK ABOUT IT

Helping White Christians Talk Faithfully about Racism

CAROLYN B. HELSEL

chalice
press

Saint Louis, Missouri

An imprint of Christian Board of Publication

Scripture quotations are directly quoted or adapted from the *New Revised Standard Version Bible,* copyright © 1989 National Council of the Churches of Christ in the United States of America. Used by permission. All rights reserved.

Cover design: Jesse Turri

ChalicePress.com

Print ISBN: 9780827200722

EPUB: 9780827200739 EPDF: 9780827200746

Printed in the United States of America

CONTENTS

What if I say the wrong thing? Is race really something that I need to talk about (I'm white)? Shouldn't I let people of color be the ones to bring it up?

Introduction

WHITE AND ANXIOUS

We're talking about *what*? Race?! If you are a white person, perhaps the anxiety of talking about race begins even with the first mention of the word *race*. That part of your brain that deals with fight-or-flight responses activates, your hands start sweating, your heart begins to beat faster, and the room seems to get warmer all of a sudden. Your whole body says to you: *This is not safe! This is not a topic I can talk about!* Maybe you've had an experience in the past that makes you uncomfortable—maybe you said something that someone else pointed out was offensive. Maybe you see protests on the streets about #BlackLivesMatter and you're not sure if talking about race means you will be asked to join a march—or, if by simply being white, you will be targeted as a racist. You've been to anti-racism workshops and diversity trainings, and nearly every time someone breaks down in tears, usually a white woman, and you don't have time for any of this. Aren't there other things we should be talking about?

What are the sources of your anxiety as you think about race? What are the memories that this subject brings up for you? If you are a perfectionist, perhaps the anxiety comes from past experiences of not knowing the right answer, of trying to do something good, only to have someone else misinterpret your actions. If you get defensive when this subject is raised, perhaps it comes out of an anxiety that you will be wrongfully accused of being racist. If you generally think of yourself as a good person, perhaps this subject creates anxiety that you will never be able to be "good enough" when it comes to race...because you are a white person.

This book is written by a white person to white people. I write this book out of my own anxiety, out of my own experiences of learning about racism and trying to find a way as a white person to join a larger movement of people working for racial justice. I'm not very good at it. I lead other white people in conversations about race; I don't lead anti-racism trainings. One of my friends works for Crossroads Anti-Racism Training Ministries, and she goes around the country meeting with organizations that want her to come and talk to them about how to become anti-racist. I don't do that. I teach preaching at a predominantly white institution in Central Texas, less than a hundred miles from where I grew up. I am not a radical.

But the movement toward greater racial justice needs more than just radicals. It needs people like you and me—people who may not consider ourselves to be very radical—to reconsider where race continues to operate in our society and in our lives, and to make a difference in the areas where we can. Not everyone can drop everything and become a full-time activist. Not everyone can work full-time doing anti-racism work. However, everyone *can* learn how to talk about race, to stay in the conversation long enough, so that when the opportunity for you to act comes, you will know what to do.

So this is a book about helping you stay in this conversation, even amidst the anxiety you may feel when talking about race. This is a book to help you talk about it with other white people.

There are plenty of people of color who can tell you about their experiences of racial discrimination, but it often comes at a great cost to them. If your own anxiety is too great when someone shares with you about experiences of racial discrimination, you may be tempted to defend rather than just listen. Also, white people—you and me—need to be responsible for our own learning and education about this subject that we've been able to avoid most of our lives.

And of course, we *could* continue to avoid it. If the anxiety is too great, we could simply walk away. You could close this book, put it down right now, and leave it on the bookshelf. You could say to yourself that you have enough problems of your own to worry about the problems other people experience because of racial discrimination. You could say all of these things and not talk about race until someone at your work or place of worship brings in somebody else to talk to you about it.

But I hope this time will be different. I hope you will read this book, and, by reading it, you will feel yourself honored and cared for, your emotions attended to, and not feel shamed for getting it wrong. I want you the reader to feel as though I understand what you are going through, and that we are going through it together. I want to walk with you so you can feel encouraged to continue on this journey wherever it may take you.

I also write as a Christian, and my faith is one of the reasons I feel compelled to write about race. When Jesus Christ came and lived among humanity, he was said to have "broken down the dividing wall" (Eph. 2:14). Two thousand years later, we are still trying to live into that world of greater unity. But the moments when I have experienced unity with others, when I have felt blessed by the gift of someone else sharing with me a bit of who they are, these have been moments of grace unfolding. When I have heard people share about their experiences of suffering, and they feel I am listening and honoring their experiences, there is a sense of communion present in these spaces. I believe God is working in the midst of these challenging conversations, and it is a gift in which we have been invited to participate. So I write out of a deep sense of gratitude for what I believe God in Christ is already doing, and what I feel like we have been allowed to join. I hope you will accompany me on this journey.

In this book, I've included stories others have shared with me. Sharing these stories is a way in which I am bearing witness to what is going on in their lives, both the pain and the joy. I will share stories from people of color and from white people, and for the most part I have kept their real names because they have expressed their willingness to have these stories shared with others. In cases in which I have not directly received someone's permission to share their story, then the experience I relate will have identifying markers removed so that they can remain anonymous.

In addition to stories, this book contains questions for reflection and discussion. Because this is a book about talking and not simply reading, I ask that you find a way to read it in conversation with someone else. At moments when I ask questions of you the reader, I hope you will be in a setting in which you can answer these questions with someone else. Perhaps as part of a Bible study or a Christian education class or a leadership training event, you could read this book together and have these conversations as a group. Let others know you are reading this book and invite them to join you. The more people joining in these conversations, the greater the possibility for understanding.

Finally, expect to feel emotions while you read and talk. That is the whole point of this book: to notice the emotional toll of having these conversations so the emotions do not derail the conversation or cause you to avoid it altogether. Expect to feel emotions, and I ask that you attend to them. If you can keep a journal while reading this book, write journal entries in which you name the feelings you are experiencing. No feeling is "bad" or "wrong." Feelings just *are*. If we ignore our feelings or try to deny them, they eventually have a way of sabotaging our efforts. So as you are reading this book, take a moment—as you need it—to check in with what you are feeling, writing down your thoughts and feelings if you can, and trust that this is part of the process. Remember that it is hard to talk about race and racism. This is a long journey, so be prepared to give yourself some grace.

The following chapters invite you to consider your own emotions and stories about race, and how those stories impact how you interpret the world around you. The first chapter will talk about how these three things—emotions, stories, and interpretation—are linked together. The next chapter focuses on the feeling of "being white," and how white people are racialized in this country in different ways. Chapter 3 looks at racial identity development theory, a way of understanding the story of how white people come to see themselves as white in a positive and anti-racist way. Chapter 4 presents many different stories about race that people have shared with me, and these stories present challenging emotions. Chapter 5 moves into the work of interpretation, and I suggest that gratitude is the lens through which we can best interpret these difficult conversations. Finally, in Chapter 6 I'll present several spiritual practices for continuing to engage in difficult conversations about race.

This book is several years in the making. As I prepare to "give birth" to this book of ideas, I pray that it will meet you where you are, encouraging you to embrace hard conversations. I have read *a lot* of books, and have written a scholarly dissertation on the subject of preaching about race in white congregations, but in many ways I had to let all of that go in order to write this book. I do not write this to prove to you that I have read some important figures in the field of critical race studies or to impress you with fancy words. I write out of a heart of gratitude, a sense that God has called me to talk about the difficult topic of race among other white people, and it is a gift I want to share with you. If you choose to receive this gift, I believe you will be led into even deeper opportunities of sharing and gratitude with the people in your community and across your city. As you engage in these conversations, know that I am praying ahead of you that they may be fruitful.

Carolyn Helsel

March 15, 2017

Chapter 1

THE WAY WE THINK ABOUT RACE

When you first hear the word *race,* what are the other words that come to mind for you? Perhaps words or phrases come to mind you have heard when talking about race with someone else. I hear the following phrases regularly when I talk about race with groups of white people: "Melting pot," "reverse racism," "post-racial," and "colorblind." Each of these phrases represents a way of interpreting race today. "Melting pot" in America implies all the ethnic differences among immigrants have "melted" into one citizenry. "Reverse racism" is what white people experience when they become targeted for their race. "Post-racial" often refers to an era where talking about race is no longer necessary or useful. And the word "colorblind" refers to someone who does not see color as racial difference. Yet each of these phrases captures a world of deeper meaning frequently missed by white people when talking about race. I will talk about each of these phrases as I have heard them in conversations with other white people.

"Melting Pot"

In an online course I teach on worship, a textbook I use focuses on diversity within one of its chapters, and a student took issue with the concept. The student felt the chapter lifted up positive elements from non-white worshiping traditions, but then disparaged the contributions of so-called "white" churches. I asked him to write out his concerns, since I had not experienced the reading the same way he had. His response included a story about race: a narrative that explained his own frustration with the current conversations around race and diversity. He said that the United States used to be a country of immigrants, where each person came and contributed the best of his or her culture, and then joined the melting pot of America. Now, he believes, persons want to come and receive the best our country has to offer, to enjoy its benefits, but not become "American." They want to retain their "otherness," using a hyphenated descriptor before the word *American*. My student said he could not understand why people would immigrate here and not want to learn our language, instead insisting that we speak their language and learn about their cultures. He agreed that we could learn something from other cultures, but argued that other cultures have something to learn from whites as well.

In this student's conversation with me, he was lifting up the model of the melting pot of cultures, a way of saying talking about race maintains divisions and prevents unity. The student believed that talking about race negatively impacted what, in his mind, was a positive experience of American cultures melting into one larger nation. His story about race was that we needed to ignore it in order to maintain the melting pot of our country.

"Reverse Racism"

In a church I served, after preaching several sermons that focused on recent high-profile cases of police shootings of African American young men, one parishioner walked out in the middle of my sermon. I later learned more about the man's frustrations: they had to do with his current work environment and colleagues. As a person in the tech industry, he worked with persons over the Internet and on the phone who were often a world away. The few colleagues who actually shared a brick-and-mortar office space with him were immigrants from other parts of the world, primarily India. He was the only white person in his office and often felt excluded by his colleagues, who would sometimes speak in other languages to one another. He saw them doing well financially and professionally, while he was still struggling to succeed in the company and overlooked for promotions. He experienced my sermons that lifted up the plight of people of color at the hands of oppressive white society as a contradiction of his own experiences, and he expected I would view him as a racist for disagreeing with me. He believed "reverse racism" took place, and felt he had experienced it himself.

In anti-racist trainings, I hear the leaders state that racism against white people does not exist, even though many white people express they have experienced it. What anti-racist trainers explain is that racism is more than feelings of being discriminated against; it is the systemic exclusion of certain groups of people from having access to opportunities based on their group membership. They highlight the history of laws that have unfairly benefited whites and how laws and patterns of discrimination become invisible social structures that perpetuate inequality.

Having a new understanding of racism as benefiting whites is important. But re-defining racism for listeners does not necessarily translate into new understanding or different interpretations of the world. White people who are told racism is systemic have no framework for understanding what this looks like in everyday life. Whites who believe reverse racism exists often have a story behind this belief, and these stories cannot be changed through logical arguments alone. Knowing the stories behind our own interpretations of race can help give us clues for how we went from seeing race one way to seeing it differently. In sharing our stories, we can begin to understand what shapes our interpretations of the world.

"Post-racial" or "Colorblind"

While leading a workshop on race and racism for a predominantly white church, I sat at a table of women during one of the small group discussions. One woman, in her 40s, spoke about her daughter, whom she had adopted from China. She expressed concern that we are still talking about race, when it seemed to her that her daughter just wanted to be seen as part of her (white) adoptive family. The woman shared that her daughter never showed interest in learning about Chinese culture or finding her birth parents, and the woman saw talking about race as negatively impacting her daughter's ability to feel she truly belonged within her adoptive family. Another woman at the table, in her 70s, still remembered signs for "whites only" above bathrooms and water fountains, and she had believed that "not seeing color" was an improvement to that former way of life. Both of the women were describing a "post-racial" America, an ideal that values "colorblindness" as a way of moving beyond our ugly racist past.

If I had recently attended a workshop on anti-racism, I might quickly respond to the three scenarios above with the following explanations: "melting pot" was only ever used by *white* immigrants as an American ideal, that what whites perceive as "reverse racism" is not the same as centuries-old systemic discrimination, and "colorblindness" cannot be a positive thing when racial prejudice continues to operate beyond our awareness. I could respond this way. I believe the words. But I cannot expect that simply stating counter-arguments will change minds. Ending racism involves more than education. People need a new framework for interpreting the world they live in. The stories they believe about racism from their own perspectives are stories that make sense to them.

In order to talk about race among persons who carry a number of different stories about this subject, we need to understand the power of stories and the connection of our stories to our understanding. Cognition—how we think—is not solely responsible for how we interpret the world in which we live. Our emotions are both influenced by our interpretation of events *and* serve to influence our interpretation of events. And our interpretation of events is most often shared in *story form*, conveying the attached emotion and color of our personal perspectives. This is why some therapists engage their clients in cognitive-behavioral therapies to help the clients deal with serious emotional concerns: how we think about the world influences our emotions, and, likewise, our emotions impact how we think about the world.

Stories and Emotions Surrounding Race

In talking about race with white people, the emotions related to whiteness impact how we see the world. When anti-racist trainers introduce the statement "racism is prejudice plus power," white persons may not see themselves as powerful—and this feeling prevents them from viewing whites as a racial group continuing to hold the greatest power in our society. The word *racism* is connected in their minds to other stories that also impact their emotional reaction to talking about it. Stories that come from the person's history, from their education or schooling, from media sources, from friends and family, all influence their emotional reactions and their interpretation of the word *racism*. When talking about race and racism, we need to tell these stories and sit with the emotions they bring up for us. White people also need to hear the stories of others who have had different experiences than their own.

To be able to join the conversation and engage meaningfully with racial injustice, we must also expand our understandings of what racism means. Culture has changed, society's racial stratification has evolved, and demographics in the United States have changed. Yet racism continues to be experienced in real and life-threatening ways for persons of color. For white persons who want to understand the phenomenon of current racism, we need to be able to recognize it, not only by bringing to mind our previous understandings of racism, but also to re-evaluate our understandings. It is necessary to broaden our own collection of stories that inform our understanding of racism, and rethink our assumptions about what racism looks like today.

The Power of Interpretation: Trayvon Martin and #BlacksLivesMatter

In the year 2012 in Stanford, Florida, a black teenager named Trayvon Martin was walking home wearing a hoodie in the rain, having just walked to a gas station to buy a drink and a bag of Skittles. On his way home, a person driving around caught sight of him and thought he looked "suspicious." That split-second interpretation sentenced Trayvon to death.

His shooter, George Zimmerman, interpreted Trayvon's presence as a threat, an interpretation that led to the confrontation that ended in Zimmerman shooting and killing Trayvon. Zimmerman had in his mind a story of assumptions about a young black man wearing a hoodie sweatshirt. The story in his mind told him that this young man was someone to fear and to suspect, and that interpretation brought on an aggressive encounter that ended with a gun shot that killed Trayvon Martin.

Zimmerman was acquitted for Trayvon's murder. The jury consisted of six women—all of whom were white, with one exception. Their interpretation of the events as the defense attorney presented them was that Zimmerman was not guilty of any wrongdoing, and that Trayvon's response to Zimmerman may have been partially responsible for his own death.

The news of Zimmerman's acquittal created outrage and sadness for many across the country who saw this verdict as another sign that black bodies were disposable. In response, a young black woman named Alicia Garza posted a "love letter to black people" in which she expressed her sadness at "how little Black lives matter." Her friend, Patrisse Cullors, created the Twitter hashtag #BlackLivesMatter. The hashtag began as a rallying cry, to say to those who looked like Trayvon, who risked losing their lives because they were automatically "suspicious," that their lives *mattered*.

In response to the "Black Lives Matter" phrase gaining support, some white people took offense. People began posted "ALL lives matter." These reactions missed the point: what the original writers were expressing is that "Black Lives Matter **Too**" because of how often they had seen black people shot without any repercussion for the shooter. The people who lifted up Black Lives Matter did so as a protest, as a cry against the injustice they witnessed on a regular basis.

A year after the Zimmerman acquittal, in the summer of 2014 in Ferguson, Missouri, a white police officer shot and killed an unarmed 18-year-old named Michael Brown. Brown's body lay in the middle of the street for four hours. As a result, three young adults began coordinating protests and freedom rides for persons to come from all over to protest what they saw as the racism exhibited in Michael Brown's death. DeRay Mckesson, Brittany Packnett, and Johnetta Elzie were among recognized leaders of the Black Lives Matter movement in Ferguson.[1] The Blacks Lives Matter movement continues to grow, bringing together groups of people across the country who see racism still at work in society and who are trying to change the systems that enable the deaths of Trayvon and Michael and others who look like them, calling for greater accountability for their deaths.

In the summer of 2016, Philando Castile was killed by a police officer after a traffic stop and responding to the requests of the officer. Protests erupted across the country. Later that week, as Dallas police officers stood by a group of Black Lives Matter protestors, a madman shot and killed five officers. While some

---

1 Jelani Cobb, "The Matter of Black Lives." *The New Yorker* (March 14, 2016). Accessed online at http://www.newyorker.com/magazine/2016/03/14/where-is-black-lives-matter-headed.

blamed the Black Lives Matter movement for the violence, investigators found no connection between the shooter and the Black Lives Matter group. Later that summer, a white man shot and killed two police officers in Iowa while they sat in their vehicle. Friends and family of police officers around the country proclaimed that "Blue Lives Matter," emphasizing the dangerous job officers take on every day to protect the lives of citizens. Meanwhile, leaders of the Black Lives Matter movement expressed their sadness and outrage at the deaths of these officers, condemning violence against the police.

There is no question that police officers have a dangerous job, and I grieve for the families of those who lose their loved ones in the line of fire. At the same time, it is not fair to compare the deaths of these police officers to the deaths of unarmed brown and black men and women. As I edit this manuscript for publication, the verdict for the officer who shot Philando Castile came back: acquittal. Do an Internet search of the list of names of people of color killed by police officers or in police custody whose deaths led to no conviction. If you as a white person were seeing this happen to people who looked like you, people who looked like your brother or sister, parent or child, how would these stories impact you emotionally? What would it feel like to have so many people who look like you killed by the police, and see court case after court case end with no conviction for the officers? Would you be enraged? And terrified?

Interpretation and Emotion

In response to the events described above, some people in our white churches are slow to attribute the root cause of these black deaths to racism. In fact, talking about racism is typically avoided by our churches. Perhaps this is to avoid controversy or because people believe that talking about race will lead to them being labeled as racists. Perhaps the subject seems too terrible to mention: the shootings of Trayvon Martin, Michael Brown, Philando Castile, and others killed by police and citizen profilers are too complicated—we would rather avert our eyes and shake our heads than say something stupid or offensive.

Our emotions play a role in our interpretations of events, as well as whether we choose to share our understandings with others. Our emotions may prevent us from saying something at all about the deaths of these and many other similar young men. Fear, anxiety, guilt, shame—these and other emotions conspire against us, urging us not to take any kind of stand. Or, we can become bold and talk about these events and ask what we can do in response. We can reach out to the members of the black community in our cities and ask how we can show our support and solidarity. But having these conversations, showing solidarity—these kinds of actions require that we be comfortable using the words *race* and *racism,* so that we can be supportive of persons who feel regularly victimized because of the color of their skin.

But part of the challenge is the intensity of the complex emotions that emerge both from ourselves and from others when we begin naming the injustice of racism. We may find ourselves feeling intensely sad, or we experience the emotions of others such as anger or frustration, and we are not always good at knowing what to do with other people's feelings, especially anger. We may take it personally. We may fear being overwhelmed by another person's sorrow and grief. We would prefer to inoculate ourselves against the deep suffering of another person.

In having conversations about race with other white people, our interpretations about race may be different from theirs. Our friends and neighbors' interpretations of race in the world may be different from our own because of their personal experiences, early learnings, or struggles. Persons' emotional reactions to talking about racism may become an obstacle. A better self-understanding of our emotions will not only help us talk with others, but it can also give us patience with one another and help us honor each other's emotions as we engage in the conversation.

Many of us white people who grew up after the 1960s believed that after the Civil Rights Movement, racism was no longer a major problem. We believed that there were still racists in extreme cases—skinheads and KKK members—but that most white people knew better than to be racist. It was socially unacceptable to be racist. It was only the result of ignorance that led to racism. So if you were not ignorant and you seemed to be relatively socially astute, then your self-perception was you were not one of "them," the racists "out there."

But to hear a different story, to learn that we ourselves have most likely said or done something that was perceived as racist by another person, or that we contribute to the system of racism, these stories make us feel bad. We are disoriented. We're not sure who we are anymore. We're not sure whether we can talk about race for fear of saying something stupid. We're not sure we can mention that we are white without sounding like we are a white supremacist. We fear being accused of racism, and we berate ourselves when we realize we have harbored racist attitudes.

The Broadway musical *South Pacific* includes a song "You've Got to Be Carefully Taught," which portrays the process of educating persons into racism. Racist beliefs are beliefs that persons learn while growing up in order to function more effectively in society. The assumption has been that if persons could be educated into racism, then they could be educated out of racism. But in changing the emotions surrounding how we interpret racism, education is not a simple process of passing information on that someone else receives and accepts as true. There are stories that have already been part of our understanding of racism that we need to better understand and try to re-narrate. There are also emotional components that have to do with recognizing oneself within the story.

There are also many whites who quickly detach from such painful history by saying: "My ancestors never owned any slaves," or, "I grew up poor and all my family members are poor—so where are these 'benefits' or 'privileges' you're talking about for us?" It can be painful for white people to talk about race, but for different reasons, depending on their personal experiences. Each person has a story.

My Story

I am white, but I would not have willingly called myself white when I was growing up in the 1980s unless I had to fill out a form requesting my race, nor did I think about being white when I felt called to ministry or went to college. But in seminary, I learned through reading books on theology written by African American women that black women still experienced racism. These women taught me that ignoring the fact that I was white was a symptom of a larger problem in society that viewed persons like me as "normal" or without a race. I discovered from talking to my peers the many ways persons of color continue to experience racism in subtle and not-so-subtle ways, and that, by ignoring my own race, I was dismissing or minimizing their experiences.

But reckoning with my own race was uncomfortable. I felt ashamed of being white and guilty for receiving unearned advantages or privileges as a result of my whiteness. I knew racism was real, but I did not want to think about myself as white. In ministry, I also encountered others like me who were white but who avoided naming themselves as white or talking about race or racism. As a preacher, I realized I needed to talk about being white, but was not comfortable discussing a subject that brought up so much anxiety and shame.

Then I came across racial identity development theory. A professor who knew I was interested in the subject of race gave me an article written by Beverly Daniel Tatum, former President of Spelman College in Atlanta.[2] The article described how a group of students who were learning about race in the classroom

---

2   Beverly Daniel Tatum, "Talking about Race, Learning about Racism: The Application of Racial Identity Development in the Classroom," *Harvard Educational Review* 62 (Spring 1992): 1–25.

were able to stay engaged in discussions when they knew in advance they were going to be uncomfortable. The teacher had discussed with the students ahead of time about the theory of racial identity development.[3] The theory is that persons come to see themselves as racialized in stages and that individuals can move toward a healthier racial self-understanding. For persons of color, that means unlearning the internalized racism they may unconsciously hold; for whites, that means understanding the legacy of racism and developing an anti-racist white identity not based on feelings of superiority.

For white persons, the stages of racial identity development begin with the experience of disorientation: the confusion and shame that white people have when they first begin learning about racism. White racial identity development then moves into a stage of "reorientation," in which whites may turn their inner negative feelings outward and onto people of color. Naming the reorientation stage helps whites become aware of their tendency to project their own negative feelings onto others. Moving beyond this tendency requires that whites stay committed to learning more about racism, even while their emotions are leading them to withdraw from the conversation. Staying engaged enables whites to continue learning about the history of racism, along with the legacy of other whites who have fought for racial justice. Then, it is possible for whites to begin building coalitions with persons of color and recognize how racism intersects with other experiences of oppression. The final stage is reached when race no longer symbolizes threat and whites can grow in greater solidarity with persons of color. More about racial identity development—for whites and for people of color—will be discussed in chapter 3. I describe it briefly here to show how my story began to change.

For me, the realization that guilt and shame are *not* the final goal was redemptive. I began to understand my emotions as necessary

---

3   Tatum cites the work of Janet Helms. See Janet Helms, ed., *Black and White Racial Identity: Research, Theory and Practice* (Westport, Conn.: Greenwood Press, 1990).

to the challenging process of learning about racism, as well as helpful to helping other whites understand that racism remains a problem. I also came to see that healthy white racial identity grows through understanding the negative feelings we feel when talking about race, and accepting them to stay engaged with the long-term process of healing and understanding.

Racial justice educator Robin DiAngelo says white people suffer from "white fragility" when it comes to encountering conversations about race.[4] She argues that the emotions of white people often get in the way of learning about the realities of racism because white people often live segregated from "racial stress," noting that when whites first experience it, they often react defensively, expressing outward anger, arguing, or withdrawing completely. We need to consider the emotions we experience while talking about race, and become able to sit with them and honor them, rather than withdrawing.

Questions for Reflection and Discussion:

Hopefully you are reading this book with someone else. Take time now to talk about some of the ideas from this chapter. What feelings emerge when you hear the topic of race raised? Do you feel nervous or frustrated? Perhaps irritated or angry? Maybe you feel sadness or guilt? Where do those feelings come from, and where do you experience them in your body? Sometimes I experience feelings in my gut, like they are sitting right on my stomach. Other times, I'm not even aware of my feelings. When that happens, I can be stuck in my head, not aware of what my body is going through, whether getting sweaty palms or a faster heart rate.

As you begin these conversations about race and racism, think about the stories that come to mind for you and name the feelings that they bring up. Pay attention to your own body in this moment. Take deep breaths. Share with someone else some of your past experiences of talking about

---

4   Robin DiAngelo, "White Fragility," *International Journal of Critical Pedagogy* 3, no. 3 (2011): 54–70.

race and racism, and name one thing you hope you will gain from this experience. Pray for one another, and also pray for all of those who experience racial discrimination. Lift up in prayer the families of Trayvon Martin, Michael Brown, Philando Castile, and the police officers shot in Dallas and Iowa. Pray for all of the people whose stories we haven't heard. Pray for God to bring the healing and reconciliation that only God can bring.

I get angry thinking you're trying to make me more politically correct. I don't see color. Why do we have to keep talking about this?

Chapter 2

FEELING WHITE

A white friend of mine is in her 60s. She knew I was writing about race and wanted to share with me some of her memories of growing up in segregated Texas. She remembers having separate water fountains and separate bathrooms. She saw a picture of a green and yellow bus in a book on Rosa Parks and told me she remembered riding in buses that looked just like that, with blacks sitting in the back of the bus and whites sitting in the front. She told me there were even separate rooms in Luby's Cafeteria restaurants. There would be a room for blacks, a room for white smokers, and a room for non-smoking whites.

> "That's just the way it was. It didn't seem right or wrong, it just *was*. We didn't know anything different. It wasn't until later, when I got my first job out of college, and I'm going to the restroom, and a black woman comes into the restroom after me. And I realized, I had never been in a bathroom with a black woman before. And this was in a time when I was working at a place where there were very few other women. I was called 'girl' and had to correct them every time!

"When I had children, the TV shows my kids would watch [in the late 1980s] often had good guys and bad guys dressed up in different colored clothes. The good guys were always wearing white and the bad guys were always wearing black. My son, watching one of these shows one day, says to me, 'Mom, all the bad guys are always black.' And I was shocked and said, 'No they are not! Did you know your housekeeper is black? Did you know your teacher is black?' And my son looks at me, mouth open, saying, 'No! I never knew!' Well, then he goes to school the next day, and I get a call from the counselor. Apparently, he had gone up to his kindergarten teacher and said, 'Ms. Thompson, did you know you were black?' And of course he didn't mean anything by it! But I had to come and explain to them what we had talked about the day before. Because, he hadn't really even noticed that she was black until that day."

My friend had never intentionally tried to be mean to black people. She never realized growing up that segregation was a bad thing, nor did she necessarily think it was a good thing. It just *was*. She did not say she was shocked or disappointed when segregation changed, just that it was different.

We all grow up believing in a world in which things are done in a certain way. You do not know the world in any other way than how it first appears to you. Then, at some point, things begin to change. At first, the change appears gradually, but in other places the change appears quickly and dramatically. The world no longer looks to you the way it once had. How do you respond?

If someone accuses you of harming others because the world operated differently when you were born, you feel offended: how could you have anything to do with that? How could you have known it hurt others when it was just the way the world *was*?

You were nice and kind to everyone you met, and you are a good person who often helps others in need. It hurts you that someone else would view you in such a negative light and attribute such mean actions to you unjustly.

White people born in white communities where segregation just *was* grew up to see drastic changes in the world. They saw persons who were not white receive greater attention and opportunities, and they witnessed great political protests and new laws passed against discrimination. Some of these changes may have affected them personally—for instance, seeing more people of color in their schools and neighborhoods and places of work. But many did not experience a significant impact on their daily lives as a result. Now, the world just *is* different. To them, it's neither bad nor good, but just the way things are now.

Trying to shame such persons into feeling guilty for having white privilege or being "white supremacists" will make no difference. They feel no guilt or shame; they have lived a relatively blameless life. Criticizing them as racists or asking them to "check their privilege" will not resonate. It will merely shut down the conversation, and make the person want to avoid talking about the subject altogether.

Have you had an experience like this? Have you felt wrongly accused of being a racist? What were your initial reactions? Looking back, do you have more insight than you did then? What do you wish would have happened differently?

Thinking about your answers to those questions will help you determine how this experience influenced the way you feel about this topic now.

Segregation and the Absence of Conversations about Race

One of the ongoing problems of race is the segregation of white people into isolated circles. Whites continue to hold power and access to opportunities that, if kept to themselves, perpetuate inequality between races. Attempts to address this segregation have been successful to an extent, but there is much more to be done. Laws to enforce desegregation led to busing students across town to attend school with different races—white kids with black kids. More white people were able to say that they personally knew people of color. But that also led to backlash and further segregation, as seen in Boston in the late 1970s. Boston's working-class neighborhoods went into an uproar when students were bused to schools in other working class neighborhoods. White parents who had money moved to the suburbs or put their children in private schools. Looking at statistics today, the situation across metropolitan areas remains largely unchanged: public schools continue to be predominantly segregated, and neighborhoods are as well.

Part of the problem was the lack of authentic relationships. White kids sitting in a classroom with a couple of black kids could say they "knew" these other children, but these relationships were often only superficial, and lasted only during school hours. Children and youth might play together on sports teams, but after the game and outside of school hours, white kids would hang out with other white kids in their neighborhood, and the black kids would hang out somewhere else. There was less interest in socializing outside the school. White kids would rarely go over to their black friends' houses on the other side of town.

White people's friendships largely remain segregated, and studies have reported that within white people's circles, very few have hosted someone of color or visited someone non-white in their home. Churches also remain largely segregated. These places of relationship—schools, neighborhoods, and churches—continue to reinforce separation.

The problem is not simply race. The deeper problem is the inability to relate across racial differences.

Responsibility vs. Response-ability

If you have a hard time feeling responsible for racism, you may have trouble considering your responsibility. If that's the case, it may be good to consider your "response-ability." To say you are responsible for something brings up feelings of defensiveness, perhaps anger, and these strong emotions make it difficult to hear others' perspectives, let alone build meaningful relationships. Often, persons sharing their frustrations about racism need you to simply hear them, not to take personal responsibility. You can be *response-able*, having the ability to respond with compassion and care, without needing to feel personally responsible.

When someone talks about their experience of being pulled over by the police in their own neighborhood for the ninth time that year, you can respond with compassion to that person's experiences and feelings of anger and sadness. Alternatively, responding by trying to explain, rationalize, defend, or otherwise dismiss their experience limits your *response-ability,* and you are less likely to build a meaningful relationship with them. They are not asking you to take responsibility for the police; they've invited you into their experience. They know this is not your common experience, and they aren't asking you to do anything about it or to make sense of it. You are not responsible for the fear or anger they feel. But you can be *response-able* by listening, believing, and accepting their experience.

Being *response-able* to anger can be particularly challenging. As a white person, listening to a person of color share about discrimination by another white person or white society in general can be difficult to hear and not interpret it as being directed at you. For example, a Latino man says white people always assume he's a foreigner or from Mexico, when in reality he's from Puerto Rico, which makes him an American citizen. You hear this, and you sense he is angry. Where does your mind go? Is it to thinking whether or not you have ever done this? Or is it to defensiveness, thinking he's being too sensitive and it's an easy mistake?

Some white people when talking about race say they "feel stupid." Maybe you didn't realize Puerto Ricans were American citizens, and now you're wondering if you should just back away from the conversation and Google information about Puerto Rico. To feel stupid is to feel inadequate, insecure. So what do you do with that? It is not helpful for meaningful relationships.

Given that you just saw his frustration that white people are not aware Puerto Ricans are citizens, you may be hesitant to say, "Wow, I didn't know that, either." You don't want his anger directed at you, and this white anxiety could prevent you from continuing the conversation. You may keep your mouth shut, feeling guilty for your own ignorance. Perhaps you felt responsible—convicted—because you were guilty of assuming Puerto Ricans were foreigners. But what if instead of letting this push you away, you focused instead on your *response-ability?* Might you be able to improve your relationship with this man?

Being *response-able* might mean you could listen to his frustration and not say anything. Perhaps being response-able would include saying "I'm so sorry—that must be really frustrating." It might include getting to know this person better and learning what his experiences have been like living between Puerto Rico and the United States. Perhaps it could mean thinking about your own education as a white American, never learning in public school history lessons about the unincorporated territories of the United States. Perhaps it means simply sitting with the anger that the other person feels, understanding that it's about something much bigger than you, and it's not in your power to do anything about it. Your response-*ability* is in your power—how you respond in the moment.

Of course this discernment and presence of mind takes practice, mindfulness. It requires being mindful of our own tendencies to react to anger with fight-or-flight rather than acceptance and peace-making. It can be important to tell yourself you are safe and this person's anger will not harm you.

Also important is to understand the role of anger in the work of justice. Anger about injustice propels us to make a difference. At the same time, anger can feel all-consuming, and so we need to take breaks from time to time from our anger. The best way to diffuse anger is to help someone feel they have been heard. If you express your anger and someone dismisses you or ignores you or tries to talk you out of your anger, they only fuel it and make it greater. But if you share your anger and they listen to you without becoming defensive, you feel heard. The issue may not be resolved, but the anger itself diffuses and the mind can begin to work again. Then you can feel free to address the action that caused the anger. The anger has served its purpose and is no longer needed.

But imagine you are known as an "angry black woman," a stereotype that many whites have toward black women. Imagine you are angry about being treated unfairly, but because of this stereotype, you cannot express your anger. If you do express your anger, you are dismissed as being an "angry black woman." So you stifle your anger, you put on a smile, and you turn the other cheek. Imagine this kind of response happening again and again. The anger, which is justified, never gets heard. The anger does not achieve its purpose. So you feel crazy, constantly avoiding your feelings and having to talk yourself down, never letting the anger speak. Imagine what might that do to your overall physical health? Your spiritual health? Your mental health?

If we were to walk in the shoes of a person of color for a day, seeing the little and big things that communicate to you that your race makes you a problem, then we would feel angry. We would feel like the world is unfair. We would want to tell someone about it. Consider your own experiences of when life has seemed unfair and unjust, and you will remember your feelings of anger.

Building relationships with people of color involves being able to respond to anger without becoming overwhelmed or afraid or defensive. Building relationships with people who have been discriminated against means believing that their experiences of discrimination are real, and that their feelings are what we would feel if we were in the same situations on a daily basis. Authentic relationships require this kind of *response-ability:* being able to hear the frustration and the pain another person has experienced, without feeling as if we need to run in and "fix it" or save them. Instead, we are called to respond by being witnesses, accompanying our brothers and sisters and supporting them in whatever ways we can.

The Problem with Political Correctness

During the presidential campaign and administration of Donald Trump, many of his supporters voiced their appreciation for his lack of political correctness—being able to "tell it like it is." I have a hunch why these supporters appreciate such candor. To have someone in the highest office say things that are offensive to certain groups, and to then get away with it by still being able to become President, shows being politically correct is not a requirement for being voted in to lead. For persons who feel they will never be "politically correct," this is freeing. They no longer have to measure up to a confusing standard of political correctness that for them was ever-elusive.

The concept of political correctness is one of evaluation: either you (or the things you say) are politically correct or not. Often the criteria for what counts as correct changes over time, so it becomes a moving target. If you are prone to saying things others deem offensive, you will resent the constant evaluation and the constant assessment that you are wrong, that you are saying the wrong thing. You may not change the way you feel, but you are being asked to use words that are less offensive in order to make them politically correct. So political correctness becomes this annoying morality code that is always telling you, "You're wrong, you're offensive, you're a bad person." Living with this kind of message for long enough will make you want to say, "To heck with political correctness," and appreciate seeing someone not politically correct being successful in the political realm.

I say all this not because I think political correctness is a bad thing. I say this because I understand how the concept can become this sense of judgment for people who are called out for not being politically correct. No one appreciates the feeling of being judged. If you are someone who lives in a part of the country where you already have a negative view about liberals in the big cities or on the coasts of the country, feeling judged by these liberals makes you even more resentful. Coastal and big city liberals acting like they are the moral exemplars and talking about other white people as ignorant and morally immature makes a person resent all this condescension. When white people are condescending toward other white people, neither group is going to change their minds about the other. No one wants to be or enjoys feeling shamed or criticized.

My Story: Growing Up White and Female

As a white person born in a Republican home, I grew up with the attitude that political correctness was a fake morality. As an evangelical Christian, I knew my faith was real and that the morality I followed had to do with my personal relationship with Jesus Christ, and no secular liberalism was going to compromise my values for the sake of the idolatry of political correctness. In a senior sermon I preached at my church as a high school student, I spoke sarcastically of the age we lived in (the late 1990s) as one in which tolerance was the highest virtue.

As a woman, I grew up assuming that I could do anything. I saw women working as associate pastors at my large mainline church. I had learned the term "femi-nazi" from overhearing Rush Limbaugh on the radio. I had the impression that people worrying about women's rights were struggling against invisible enemies, ones they no longer needed to fight. Feminism was not necessary. When I heard my mom was taking a course at a local university on women and gender, I asked "Why? Feminism is over—why talk about it anymore?" As a teenager, I knew everything. (I even asked my friend why her parents had put up a refrigerator magnet that said "Ask a teenager, while they still know everything." I asked her why grown-ups thought this was funny "because we *do* know everything!")

I went to a small liberal arts college in the Pacific Northwest, because I had heard that this school had a great religion department, and when I visited the campus they seemed to share the same evangelical, passionate faith that made me feel at home. The classes I took helped me to think about my faith without deconstructing it, and many of my fellow classmates were also committed to pursuing some form of ministry after college. Many students spent their Saturday nights serving the homeless and bringing food to people living downtown with limited resources. It was an inspiring place to grow in community with others who shared my sense of faith.

I began to feel a bit disconcerted when some of these same peers let me know they didn't think God called women to preaching ministry. God surely calls women to "all" forms of ministry, they assured me, but preaching was reserved specifically for men, as it said in the Bible. These peers were ones I looked up to as examples of Christian faith, knowing the Bible better than I did, expressing their faith through service to the poor downtown. One of these peers I even had a crush on; he was so smart, and such a faithful Christian—how could he be wrong? I felt I needed to justify my sense of calling to the preaching ministry to this man I respected.

A sense of calling is a subjective thing. You cannot point to an external event others could have witnessed and say, "There—that was a sense of call, don't you see it?" Instead, it is a personal experience, possibly misinterpreted, open to questioning and doubt. I could tell you exactly where I was when I felt the call to ministry, and you might shrug your shoulders and say, "Eh. You can't be sure." No, I can't be sure. And as a woman, my call was now suspect by these other faithful Christians who read a Bible that told them God doesn't call women to preach.

I felt called to preach on a Sunday afternoon when I was 15 years old. My youth director was driving me home from a church event, and as we drove down Highway 281 crossing over the Olmos Basin, he asked if I had ever considered going into ministry. I explained that, just recently, in fact, I had thought about it. I was about to finish my sophomore year in high school, so I was thinking seriously about college. I realized blind ambition was not sufficient for choosing a college; I didn't want to apply to Yale or Harvard simply because of the name recognition. I wanted to apply where I would be best prepared for what God wanted me to do. But what did God want me to do? As I was thinking about this, the image of a preacher in a pulpit came into my mind, and I immediately shut it out. I told my youth director about this, saying I knew I couldn't be called to ministry because I wasn't a good enough example and I wasn't a good public speaker. He told me about Moses and Paul, both of whom resisted God's call—but God empowered them anyway.

There, in that conversation, I experienced a call to ministry. As we pulled up to my house and I got out of the car and stood on the edge of my driveway, I had felt everything inside me saying "YES." I knew what I was supposed to do. I knew what God was calling me to do.

But a few years later, in college, that experience was called into question. How could I be sure God was really calling me to preach? Perhaps it was some other form of ministry God had in mind for me. I later learned that my youth director had changed denominations, now working in an Orthodox church, and he was no longer sure that God called women to ministry as preachers. If the very person who had helped me hear God's call was no longer sure women were called to preach, then how could I claim any certainty that God was calling me?

I tried to rationalize my way out by learning as many arguments as I could for women's ordination, as well as the arguments against it. In a college course on Christian doctrine, we were invited to take sides on theological debates and argue for a particular point of view. I chose to debate against women's ordination in order to better understand the rational arguments behind this perspective. Unfortunately, I did an excellent job. I was so thorough in my research and argumentation that I ended up convincing the class. I was devastated.

I met with one of my professors from the religion department, sharing that I was struggling with the biblical passages that stated women were to "remain silent" and were not supposed to teach or preach. I hoped he would give me encouragement and insight and help me regain a sense of confidence God had called me. All I remember of our conversation was him telling me: "I'm glad you are struggling with these texts. I think more people today need to really wrestle with this." I was heartbroken. If all I could do was wrestle with these texts, I knew I would lose. These texts and all the years of Christians thinkers interpreting them a certain way were sure to overpower me. I simply wasn't strong enough. And as a woman, I was supposed to be submissive and obedient, to find my power in service. Wrestling and overpowering the arguments was unthinkable for me as a woman. There was no way I could read these texts and take them seriously and still say I was called by God to preach.

Discouraged, but still sensing God leading me to ministry, I applied to seminary. I discovered I could graduate a year early from college, and having taken all the courses for my religion major, I felt it was time to move on. I graduated early, and packing up my belongings, I drove a rental truck across the country to begin graduate studies for ministry.

Seminary exposed me to the ideas of feminist theologians. I learned about internalized oppression, how the devaluing of some groups by others can lead to self-doubt. These thinkers helped me consider that the root of sin was not always "pride," but could also be its opposite: the harmful belittling of one's self. They suggested that how we talk and think about God impacts how we talk about God's creation, including humans. If we talk about the story of creation emphasizing God's curse on Eve after she ate the fruit in the garden of Eden, then we will talk about women as though they were cursed. If we talk about God always in male language and imagery, then we may talk only about men as being representatives of God. How we view God impacts how we view ourselves and one another.

I learned that talking about God in male and female imagery is important, and this was not just about being politically correct. Female imagery for God is there in the Bible, and even from the beginning in Genesis. "Then God said: 'Let us make humankind in our image...' / So God created humankind...; / *male and female* [God] created them" (Gen. 1:26–27). If both men *and* women are created in God's image, then God's image must include both the masculine and the feminine. Women could not be made in God's image if there was nothing like women within God. This is more than political correctness; this is theological accuracy. This is making sure that the ways we refer to God help us to see God in more people than just the male population.

And in reading about feminist theology, I also began learning about racism. I realized that in all my upbringing within the Christian church and a Christian college, no one had pointed out the sin of racism as something I needed to watch out for or repent from. It was never talked about as a source of humanity's alienation from God and from one another. I never heard racism spoken about as a demonic force that weaves its way through our culture and institutions. Such condemnation was reserved for issues of sexuality or other "cultural values," but never racism.

In seminary, I also learned that by focusing only on "feminist" concerns, many white women were ignoring the experiences of black women who could not choose to advocate for their gender without also advocating on behalf of their race. Black women were suffering from the same sexist barriers white women faced, but with the added obstacles of racism. The frustrations black women had toward white women involved feeling white feminists did not care about the experiences of black women, or how women of all colors need to work together to work for justice. Even recently, when calling for a "Day without Women," white women who advocated for all women to boycott their places of employment for a day seemed unaware of the job insecurity poor women face; calling on them to boycott their jobs for a day could lead to them losing their only access to a paycheck. In particular women working in low-paying jobs whose immigrant status makes them ineligible for any of our social safety nets cannot afford to lose the income they need to provide for their families. Working for equality must continue, but it takes different forms depending on one's social location and access to resources. Those of us with great access must advocate on behalf of those who have less.

The Problem with Political Correctness, Part 2

Some may say that worrying about whether our efforts at working for justice are exclusive or insensitive is a divisive distraction. Perhaps someone may think the critique against white feminists as being racist or classist is an example of political correctness run amok. If progressive liberals can't quit fighting about who is most liberal, then why inflict the rest of society with this unattainable standard?

However, the problem with political correctness is with its assumed goal: not offending. If our only goal is avoiding offense, or speaking so that people from across the political spectrum will not be offended by what we are saying, then we are working toward a weak goal. Not to offend others is a very low bar. It is easy to meet this bench mark by simply saying the things you know others want to hear.

A much loftier goal is the call of Jesus Christ to "love one another. Just as I have loved you, you also should love one another" (Jn.

13:34). Loving others means much more than not offending someone. To aim to not offend is the bare minimum, but it says nothing of your intention to love that person. Love requires something greater: to actually *know* that other person, to *seek* to know them and to love them. It means having compassion for how that person has suffered, and to desire the best for them. Rather than simply avoid offending another, love means actively finding out ways to honor and care for them.

When Jesus says to his disciples "love one another. Just as I have loved you, you also should love one another," he is saying this just after Judas Iscariot has left to betray him. Judas was one of his disciples, and he sold Jesus to the authorities in exchange for a reward. Yet Jesus knew Judas would do this. And even though Jesus knew this about Judas, he still cared for Judas. In the scene before these verses in John 13, Jesus washes the disciples' feet—*all* of the disciples' feet, including those of Judas Iscariot. Jesus was showing love, not by avoiding offense, but by actively loving Judas in spite of the betrayal he knew would come.

Love requires more from us than polite language or saying the right thing. Love requires we learn about one another and care for one another even in the midst of our disagreements. "Just as I have loved you, you also should love one another."

We love one another because God first loved us, and because in Christ we have been able to know God. In the first letter of John, the author writes about love and how this love comes from God's love for us:

> There is no fear in love, but perfect love casts out fear; for fear has to do with punishment, and whoever fears has not reached perfection in love... We love because he first loved us. Those who say, 'I love God,' and hate their brothers or sisters, are liars; for those who do not love a brother or sister whom they have seen, cannot love God whom they have not seen. The commandment we have from him is this: those who

love God must love their brothers and sisters also. (1 Jn. 4:18–21)

Love casts out fear. Being afraid of being "politically correct" will not help you love your neighbor. Being afraid of groups of people will not help you love your neighbor. If you are afraid of Muslims because of a terrorist who claims they are acting out of faith in Islam, you will not be able to love your Muslim neighbor. If you are afraid of all immigrants because of news reports that an immigrant committed a crime, you will not be able to love your immigrant neighbor. What you know about one member of a group does not mean you know about every person in that group. But knowing your neighbors and asking them to help you understand them better will help you to love them.

Being politically correct isn't the goal. The goal is love. The goal is building relationships. The goal is working together to make the world a better place, to care for those who are widowed or orphaned, to feed the hungry, to clothe the naked. The goal is something much bigger than political correctness.

But sometimes what is known as "political correctness" is also a sign of knowing someone, of knowing how they prefer to call themselves, of knowing their history and what has caused them pain in the past. To know what words to use around a person means you know that person and care about how words impact them. It demonstrates sensitivity and thoughtfulness.

Questions for Reflection and Discussion:

Has anyone ever made accommodations for you that made you feel cared for? Has anyone ever asked you how you wanted to be addressed, or treated you with respect? If so, then you know how it feels when another person is sensitive and thoughtful toward you. On the other hand, do you know what it feels like when someone calls you a name that hurts your feelings or makes you feel disrespected? Was the person intentionally trying to hurt you? Whether or not they hurt you on purpose, words and names can still give us pain. What is the nicest thing someone has ever said to you? Why did you appreciate it?

If you are journaling, take a moment to write about your thoughts and feelings after reading this chapter. What have been some of your experiences of "feeling white"? What feelings are brought up for you when you hear these stories? Share with someone your story of coming to notice race and its impact on your life. How do parts of our identity (our gender, for example) impact how we understand ourselves as racialized in society? Have you felt "othered" in some way because of who you are? How does this connect with your racial identity? If you are meeting in a group, close with prayer, asking God for an increased capacity for loving others where they are, including yourself.

I feel stupid when we talk about race. I have friends who are people of color and who don't want to talk about race, so why should we? But it's not my fault! I am not a racist.

Chapter 3

MAPPING RACIAL
IDENTITY DEVELOPMENT

Have you ever come across an idea that helped you make sense of the world? Can you remember learning something from a book or in school that gave you a sudden "aha!" feeling? Sometimes, particular phrases stick with us, putting things into perspective when we encounter stressful situations. For me, one such "aha" moment came when learning about racial identity development theory.[1]

All of us go through different stages as we learn to see ourselves as someone of a particular race, and understanding these stages can help us move into greater awareness of ourselves as racialized by society. Such awareness helps us identify areas for personal growth.

This theory emerged from developmental psychology, which considers how a person's inner life matures and develops over

---

1 See Beverly Daniel Tatum, "Talking about Race, Learning about Racism: The Application of Racial Identity Development in the Classroom," *Harvard Educational Review* 62 (Spring 1992): 1–25 and Janet Helms, ed., *Black and White Racial Identity: Research, Theory and Practice* (Westport, Conn.: Greenwood Press, 1990).

time. Erik Erikson, Jean Piaget, and Lawrence Kohlberg are among the earliest developmental psychologists, who studied how persons mature from infancy to late adulthood, marking crucial moments of identity formation. Teachers and parents may learn about developmental theories to help teach children more effectively and understand what child developmental stages look like. Similarly, from this, there has grown a "faith development" theory to talk about how a person's faith and images of God change over time.[2]

Racial identity development focuses on how each individual comes to see him- or herself as racialized by society. I use the word *racialized* intentionally, which refers to how persons are categorized into separate races, since how society categorizes persons changes over time. For example, Eastern Europeans were not "white" when they first immigrated in great numbers to America in the early 20th century. At some points in history persons from Arab countries have been considered "white," and at other times "not-white." Laws at times have deemed persons with "one drop" of African blood to be "black," even if a person was white-appearing.

The way we talk about skin color is a social construct—people with different skin colors are not separate races, but considered part of different groups by a history of racialization. A person has no power over how society racializes him or her, but one's own *"racial identity"* refers to how that person internalizes and responds in society as a result of being racialized. In other words, "being racialized" and "racial identity" come from two different directions. When persons are *racialized,* society has told them they are of a particular race, but a person's *racial identity* is something he or she personally claims.

A woman who grows up in a home where her mother is white, and her father is a light-skinned African-American may unconsciously

---

2   James Fowler, *Stages of Faith: The Psychology of Human Development and the Quest for Meaning* (New York: HarperCollins, 1995).

identify as white. Later in her childhood, someone may ask if she is black or tells her she is black. So the young woman has been racialized by being told she is black. Meanwhile, her racial identity goes through changes. At one point, she sees herself as white, and later, as black. Racial identity has more to do with how an individual views his or her own race, and racialization has more to do with how *other* people view your race, how society has categorized you.

Similarly, white people who have grown up "colorblind" may not see themselves as white. They may view themselves as not having any color, of just being "normal," of not having a race. But in society, they are racialized as white. They are seen as white by others, and they are treated as white, which historically has given them greater advantages and benefits than persons who are seen as not-white and who are treated differently as a result.

Of critical importance here is recognizing what racial identity can help you understand about your own emotions as you learn about race and racism. If you can better understand what you are going through, you can have a better sense of where these conversations are going and what you can expect. Racial identity development lays out a map of sorts—not that it tells you how to get from point A to point B, but it will tell you what kinds of territory you may pass through on your way toward anti-racism. This is a journey. It is not a matter of waking up and saying, "I am not a racist." It is a process of learning more about how we got to where we are now, paying attention to the subtle ways we already notice race without realizing it, and having an idea of what we can do to keep learning and growing as white anti-racists.

That was the most helpful insight from racial identity development for me: that shame and guilt were not the end goals. Every time I learned about racism, and as I began to see myself as white, I kept feeling guilty and ashamed. And that was not a pleasant feeling. I knew I wanted to be able to talk about race and racism with other white people, but I did not want to perpetuate the same feelings these conversations had left with me. And racial identity development says those feelings are not the stopping point. Those feelings may be something you experience along the way, but noticing them and paying attention to them and saying to yourself, "This is not the goal; this is not where I stop," can help you persevere in learning and growing into greater awareness of and compassion for people who experience racial discrimination.

So just what are the stages that racial identity development lays out? Well, it depends if you are a "person of color" or "white." Persons of color have their own stages that are different from those of white people. Because persons of color have been racialized as minorities and as non-white, their experiences of coming to see themselves as being a particular racial identity will be different from those of whites coming to see themselves as white.

Rather than tell you what all the stages are, I often find it more helpful to tell a couple stories. One is about a young black girl, and the other is about a young white boy—how each of them comes to see themselves as "black" or "white." You may be able to relate to some of what they go through, but you do not necessarily need to have had their experiences to go through these stages. These stories are both made up, but I have pulled details from real stories I have witnessed. Listen as a way of understanding the processes.

Ashley's Story

The first story is about a young black girl I'll call Ashley. Ashley is a beautiful and happy girl, raised in a bi-racial family in which her mother is white and her father is black. She lives with both her parents and is an only child. Her parents live in a predominantly white neighborhood in a wealthy suburb, so most of her classmates at school are white.

STAGE 1: PRE-ENCOUNTER

This beginning stage of her racial identity development is known as "pre-encounter," which means she has not yet had any encounter in which the color of her skin makes her someone of a particular "race," or any negative associations with being someone with brown skin. But she may unconsciously receive negative messages about having brown skin from the culture in which she is growing up. Because of these often-subtle messages, she internalizes negative stereotypes about people with brown skin from the dominant white society without anyone yet communicating these negative stereotypes directly.

Before she is three, she has already noticed her skin color is different from her mother's, and her parents both celebrate her and talk to her about how differences in people make them beautiful. Even though her parents have told her she is beautiful, Ashley has picked up in subtle ways from her classmates in pre-school that being brown is *not* beautiful.

One day, as her Pre-K class is coloring a picture of a girl, the children all pick colors from the available markers and crayons on the table. Ashley is left with a brown crayon that another child has passed over in order to reach for the peach-colored crayon. Ashley says aloud: "I hate brown. Brown is ugly. I don't want to use brown for my girl." No one may have said anything to her directly about brown being ugly, but she has internalized this value judgment. The teacher tries celebrating all the lovely things that are brown: chocolate and cinnamon, hot cocoa and good soil. But Ashley remains determined to color the girl in her picture a shade of pink.

STAGE 2: ENCOUNTER

Ashley is now in kindergarten at the local school. One day after school, a group of girls are jumping onto a rotating merry-go-round on the playground. Ashley runs around and tries to jump on with them. All of the girls are white, and one of them pushes

Ashley off the merry-go-round, telling her, "Only white girls allowed." Ashley ignores the girl and tries again, unsuccessfully, to join the group. She gets tired of this and runs away to do something else.

Ashley's father, who is black, sees this and is unsure what to do. He is angry and wants to tell the other little girls' parents what he has just seen, but he does not want to call attention to Ashley if she has not brought it up to him. He is also the only black parent on the playground, and he doesn't want the other parents to stereotype him as an "angry black man," so he tries to let it go.

Ashley runs over to her dad a little while later and says she wants to go home. She seems sad, and her father asks if anything happened on the playground that made her sad. She tells him about the girls saying she couldn't join them because she wasn't white. Ashley's dad experiences great sadness and shares with his daughter some of the things he heard growing up from other kids. He tries to explain to Ashley why some groups of people think they are better than other people, and how she is not alone in what she went through.

This stage of racial identity development for people of color is known as "encounter," and it begins with the experience of racial discrimination. There may be other experiences of discrimination that are not obviously racial, but at some point the individual realizes the discrimination is taking place because of the color of her skin. The person realizes they are part of a targeted racial group. Rather than just seeing herself as an individual, Ashley begins seeing herself as part of a larger group of people who are "not white" and learns she is seen as part of this other group even though she shares much in common with the white girls.

Ashley may go back and forth between these two stages, in that she may forget about these encounters and return to a kind of unconscious acceptance of the subtle messages about race that she receives every day. She may continue to internalize negative feelings about herself. On the occasions that she again experiences explicit racism, she remembers she is not alone, seen as part of this group of "others." Each time this happens, she gets angry and sad but does not have a way to deal with her feelings, and so she develops a poor self-image.

STAGE 3: IMMERSION

In this third stage, Ashley's parents become more intentional in talking to her about the Civil Rights Movement. She reads books about Martin Luther King Jr. and Rosa Parks, and she learns about the struggle for social justice. Her mom helps her to see that not all white people were against Civil Rights, and there are white people today who are working against racism. Her dad tells her about the leaders of several social justice movements, including Caesar Chavez and Ida B. Wells-Barnett.

Ashley begins seeing a lot more of the struggles that people who look like her have had to endure, and seeing their experiences makes her feel braver, knowing others have gone through what she is going through. She is starting to internalize a sense of pride in who she is—knowing she may have to endure people's racism, but she has the strength of women and men who have come before her. Ashley feels proud of being brown, and she sees lots of examples of beautiful brown people in the books and videos her parents share with her.

Ashley also begins to notice the negative self-image she had as coming from this history of racism. She realizes she does not need to believe the messages that come across in subtle ways. She can feel proud of who she is and know she is beautiful and smart. She also realizes she has to actively remind herself of this when she spends time with her white friends who can say things that hurt her feelings.

Her parents have raised her in this predominantly white neighborhood because the schools were rated the highest in the city. But because of her experiences with some of her white friends, Ashley's parents are wondering whether they should move to a part of town that has more diversity. They look for ways to surround her with people who look like her so she does not have to work so hard to feel good about herself. Having positive examples and messages about who she is can help her develop into the strong and healthy young woman she is becoming.

Ashley eventually decides to attend a Historically Black College or University (an HBCU). She surrounds herself with other black people who are passionate and smart and who never make her feel like she is "other." Her time in college is full of happy memories and a growing awareness of who she is. She participates in rallies in the local city when an unarmed black man is shot by the police. She shares her experiences of racial discrimination with others to educate them that racism is still very real in the 21st century.

STAGE 4: INTERNALIZATION

This next stage is called "internalization" because it involves an individual's racial identity becoming internalized through the positive experiences of being with others of a similar racial background. Ashley has a clearer sense of her identity even when she is not surrounded by people who look like her. She is able to develop close relationships with people from different backgrounds and sees how their struggles are similar. At this stage, she is also able to begin building coalitions with members of other oppressed groups.

After college, Ashley goes to law school to become a civil rights lawyer. Her law school is very diverse, and she finds she has a different set of friends than she had either growing up or during her college years. Some of her friends are queer, some of them have disabilities, and the racial make-up of her group includes whites and blacks, as well as Latino/as and Asian Americans.

Among this new group of friends, she is aware of other issues facing oppressed groups in society. One of her queer friends, who is white, shares with her the struggle he had gaining acceptance from his family when he came out as gay. Her Latino/a friends tell her about their fear of the discrimination their parents' face. One of them has parents who are undocumented, and, under the new president, they are afraid that one day they will be gone and have no idea how to get in touch with them if their parents are deported by Immigration and Customs Enforcement officials. Another friend who is Asian American relates to Ashley how frequently she is asked: "Where are you from?" and, "Are you an international student?" even though she and her family have lived in the United States for several generations. Another friend of hers has a disability; she struggles with mental illness and worries she will be discriminated against at work. All of these friends remind Ashley that the struggle for equal protections and respect is a long and wide one. As she begins her work as a civil rights lawyer, she takes these lessons she has learned from her colleagues and her studies to make a difference in the world.

STAGE 5: COMMITMENT

This marks the last stage of racial identity development for people of color, and involves an internal commitment that all persons are equal and deserving of respect and fair treatment. The individual seeks to make a difference by committing to address injustices that are experienced by one's own racial group as well as by other oppressed groups. The person is able to translate into action the positive understanding of one's own racial identity in order to work on behalf of others. The person sustains this commitment over time.

Ashley pursues her career as a civil rights lawyer and finds a deep sense of fulfillment in being able to help people feel valued. She finds her work very rewarding, though also very draining at times. It takes an emotional toll on her to listen to the stories of what others have experienced, and it is discouraging when she loses some of the cases she takes on. However, by attending to her own emotional well-being and caring for herself, she is able to sustain a long career. She raises her own children aware of the injustices some people experience, and in both her family and her work life she feels she is fulfilling her vocation to love and serve others.

Ashley's story is not unique. It tells us that people need to be able to feel positively about themselves, and, when they are in touch with their own pain and struggles, they are more able to connect with the pain and struggles of others, even those very different from them.

I share Ashley's story to demonstrate that people of color do not automatically wake up aware of their need for a positive racial identity or with a positive racial identity already intact. It can take years of suffering through racial discrimination before someone finally is able to stop internalizing that hate and/or negativity. People of color have to work at a positive racial identity when they are constantly bombarded with the history of negative stereotypes about themselves.

While the struggle is not the same, white people also need to develop a positive racial identity. This is not because white people experience racial discrimination, but because they do not know how to be "white" apart from this negative history of inflicting racial discrimination onto people of color. It is important for white people to be able to address racism by understanding first what it means to be white, and then be able to understand other ways that a person can be "white" within this history. There are plenty of examples of terrible white people, and there are plenty of examples of white people who allowed things to happen by being silent or standing by while terrible things happened.

But white people also need to know that there have been and still are white people who actively work for justice alongside those who have been discriminated against. It is important for white people to have positive role models for what it means to be white. That is the only way that white people can see themselves in a positive way apart from the white supremacist view that says white people are superior and good. To counteract that narrative, white people need to know about ways that whites can resist the narrative of white supremacy and still feel good about being "white."

This feeling good about being white has nothing to do with the illusions of racial superiority, and everything to do with how we can use what gifts and influence we have to make a difference on others' behalf. Let's look at what that process might entail by learning about Max.

Max's Story

Max grew up in the same neighborhood as Ashley. They were in some of the same classes in elementary school, but besides the few birthday parties to which all the kids in the class were invited, Max spent no time with Ashley outside of school. Besides Ashley, there were a few other children of color in Max's class, but he did not spend time playing with any of them.

Max had a few close friends through elementary school, and all of them looked like him: white, blond, and blue-eyed. Max didn't consciously hold any racist beliefs; he didn't choose his friends just because they were white. They merely all had things in common. They all loved baseball and biking and Pokemon cards. Their parents were all friends, and they lived just around the block from one another. At home, none of these boys' parents talked about race. It never seemed an important issue to address. Max and his friends all had parents who grew up thinking it was impolite to talk about race, and they brought up their children without reference to race in the hopes of raising them to be colorblind.

STAGE 1: CONTACT

At first, Max and his friends were in the earliest stage of racial identity development for white people, a stage known as "contact." At this stage, the white person does not have any real engagement with people of color. If they know someone of color, they do not have a close relationship with that person, or that person may be employed in the home as housekeeper. Because there is no discussion of race at home, the white person does not see "race" as a significant category for him or her. They may be aware of some of the history of racism in the United States, but largely assume that this part of history no longer has any meaning for the present.

If Max hears about a person of color expressing racial discrimination, he may wonder whether the person of color is misinterpreting it. Max may feel that persons of color are just more sensitive and would be better off if they were less sensitive. If asked if he is "white" or has a race, he most likely says, "I'm just American." He may avoid conversations about racism, assuming that such discussions have no significance for him.

Because of the unconscious way in which Max is white, he is unable to engage in meaningful conversations with persons who experience race as a label that impacts them on a daily basis. He doesn't feel race impacts him directly, and, because of that, he's not likely to engage in conversations about race. He senses it is a challenging subject, and to prevent himself feeling uncomfortable, he avoids the subject altogether and hopes that by ignoring race, racism will lessen over time.

STAGE 2: DISINTEGRATION

Max spends most of his growing up years in this first stage of "contact." He knows a few non-white students, and he plays on sports teams with them, but at the end of the day, he never invites them to his house or vice-versa. As a high school student, he notices many of the black students sit together in the cafeteria, and he sits at a table with his all-white group of friends. In his classes, he has students from a number of different racial backgrounds—some who are Indian, others who are Korean American, and another who is Chinese, he thinks. The guy he thinks is Chinese is sitting next to him in class one day, and Max tells him a joke: "What do you call it when an egg goes down a hill? An egg roll." Max smiles, thinking his classmate will think his joke is funny. Instead, the guy gets up and moves to another seat. Max is confused—what did he say? He was just trying some small talk. Max avoids talking to that student again.

Later in the school year, the counseling office hosts a diversity education event for students who apply. They get to miss a day of school to meet off-campus for a day of learning about diversity. Max is all for missing regular school, so he signs up. When he gets there, the presenter starts talking about "white privilege" and the way racism benefits white people even without their knowing it. It is a long day and Max learns a lot, but he feels really conflicted. Max was not sure what he'd signed up for, but this was not going well. The things he was hearing were making him uncomfortable—like all of a sudden he was a bad guy. He thought back to the egg roll joke he had made in class the other day. Was that racist? He hadn't thought so. After all, he loved Asian stuff. He grew up on Asian manga cartoons and Pokemon cards. How could he be racist?

This stage is called "disintegration" because it presents a challenge to a person's previously unchallenged positive view of oneself. Before this stage, the white person did not consciously think he or she was racist. Now, he or she is confronted with the message that they may be perceived as being racist even if that was not their intent. This confrontation creates a number of difficult emotions, including anger or defensiveness, as well as guilt or shame. The person feels conflicted by the reality that something he or she said was perceived as racist. This creates internal confusion and distress. There is a feeling of cognitive dissonance between how the person views him or herself and the way they are perceived by others.

STAGE 3: REINTEGRATION

After attending this event on diversity at his school, Max feels several different emotions. One is that he feels overwhelmed by all this new information. He did not know about the experiences of people of color or persons from other religious faiths who have been targeted for their faith or appearance. He feels overwhelmed and unsure of what he can possibly do about it all. He also feels a bit guilty, since as a white person who is a Christian, he does not experience discrimination on the basis of his skin color or his religious faith. Based on the things he heard in the diversity meeting, he has a lot of privilege to not experience these things, and being privileged in that way feels bad.

But Max does not like feeling bad about himself. Max has had healthy self-esteem growing up, he has been confirmed in his church, and sees himself as a moral guy. He resents the idea that somehow he has been "complicit in injustice" as the diversity training told him. How could he be getting it so wrong when he has been such a good person his whole life? Instead of feeling bad about himself, he starts to have bad feelings toward the people who presented this diversity event. "The student leaders and workshop facilitators are the ones who don't know what they're talking about," he thinks to himself. "Sure, bad things have happened in the past, but I'm no racist." He finds himself avoiding anything that has to do with the word *diversity* in the future. He thinks it is a waste of his time and that it's just trying to make him feel bad about himself. "That's not for me," he says. "I'm sure there are other people who need to hear that, but not me."

This stage of white racial identity development is known as "reintegration" because the individual reintegrates previously held understandings about themselves, ignoring messages they have heard about ongoing racism. The individual cannot hold onto the negative feelings that such conversations bring up, so he or she avoids the conversations and turns the negative feelings outward onto others. The white person may notice that he or she now has conscious thoughts about people of color that are negative. The white person may think that people of color are too focused on being the victims, or aren't taking enough responsibility for themselves. These ideas allow the white person to maintain one's prior understanding of oneself: "I'm a good person. There's no reason why I should feel bad on your behalf. If you want me to feel bad, then it's your problem, and something must be wrong with you."

The stage known as reintegration is obviously not a positive step. It's not a move forward. This stage is included within the process of white racial identity development because white people should expect to feel it. It is difficult to feel the feelings that come up when talking about race and racism, and there is a tendency to project those negative feelings about ourselves back onto other people. Those not aware of this stage may end here and avoid further growth. But knowing this is a predictable part of the development toward a healthy and positive white racial identity can help us stay engaged and have compassion for ourselves. If we can recognize our own tendencies to push our negative feelings onto others, rather than acting on those feelings, we can accept them and keep them to ourselves, trusting that as we stay engaged in the process they may transform into something else.

STAGE 4: PSEUDO-INDEPENDENT

The name of this stage captures the tentative nature of this forward movement. As the person gains a bit of independence from the earlier understanding of oneself as "normal" (not racialized), the person begins to learn more about what it means to be white in today's society. The stage includes the prefix "pseudo-" because it is a false independence. One is still stuck in understanding whiteness as the former innocence and ignorance one grew up with. The person is not yet fully ready to have genuine relationships with people of color, and the symptoms of racist beliefs still are present. But the person begins to think through what racism looks like today and understands it on an intellectual level. The person begins to accept that they are "white," even though this does not come easily or comfortably. Let's look at what is happening with Max at this stage.

Max goes away to college and, while he is there, a police officer shoots and gravely wounds an unarmed black student. The entire college campus is upset. The Black Student Caucus is out protesting on the streets in front of the school, and students of all colors have joined in the march with signs and solidarity. Max sees all of this happening and is not sure what to do. He hears his white roommate talking to a black friend, and the white roommate is saying, "I know—I've never been pulled over by the police and treated that way. There's no way that would have happened to me." His white roommate seems aware of the different treatment he receives from police than the black student. The fact that the victim of the shooting did not have any weapon makes Max incredulous. *How could this happen?* He wants to think the victim did something wrong or acted aggressively toward the police officer. He wants to believe there is some justification for the shooting. But the more he hears about the event and sees the grief of the students on his campus, he starts to wonder. He thinks to himself, "I have a lot to learn."

STAGE 5: IMMERSION

Max signs up for a class the next semester on Black Literature. He reads novels he never read in high school by Toni Morrison and Zora Neal Hurston, James Baldwin and Ralph Ellison, Frantz Fanon, Chimamanda Ngozi Adichie, and Chinua Achebe. These books make him learn of a life so different from his own. He reads Ta-Nehesi Coates and learns how far we still have to go when it comes to giving everyone a fair and equal chance to succeed. He watches PBS specials on *The Freedom Riders* and sees the white men and women who also risked their lives and well-being to sit at lunch counters with black or brown sisters or brothers. He watches the James Baldwin documentary *I Am Not Your Negro* that came out in theaters, and Max notices how similar things are between the things Baldwin wrote about and the things Max is seeing on the news today. Max begins to sense that he can get involved in some way, though he's not sure how.

This stage of white racial identity development involves immersing oneself in a historical understanding of the events and attitudes that led up to where we are today in terms of continuing racial inequality. The white person begins to read about other whites who also fought for civil rights and who continue to fight on behalf of all people who are oppressed. The white person begins to see that they can be part of this bigger story—not because they are needed as a "white savior," as is so often presented in the movies—but because they are called to be an ally, a coworker, a fellow human working for all of humanity to be recognized as fully human. The person at this point may realize the need to return to their own white community to raise awareness of ongoing racism there.

STAGE 6: AUTONOMY

This stage is called "autonomy" because the white person is no longer tied to traditional expectations of what it means to be white. They do not refuse the label "white," and it does not cause discomfort to claim their racial identity as white. The person is aware of the unfair advantages given to whites in this country, and also aware that simply being aware of white privilege does nothing to change the system that unfairly advantages whites. Because of this, the white person finds ways to actively raise awareness of racial discrimination and inequality, using what influence they have to try and widen the circle of people who will commit to addressing ongoing racism. The person at this stage also sees how whiteness and racism are interconnected with other forms of oppression involving gender, class, ability, citizenship status, sexual orientation, etc., and the person works to build coalitions with others who are also working on addressing injustice. The person seeks to learn about other cultures and communities, and values diversity in their place of work and neighborhood. Diversity of any kind no longer poses a threat.

At the same time, with any of these stages, this is not a finished project. It is not something that the white person is "done with." Instead, future experiences and opportunities challenge the person and require going back through earlier stages to accept these experiences in a growth mindset. For instance, the person may be criticized for saying something offensive, and again the person experiences the earlier stages of disintegration and reintegration, until finally accepting the accusation and learning from it. There are plenty of opportunities for persons to make mistakes in the work for justice! The goal is to continue to have humility and to be aware that none of us have "arrived," so that we can keep learning and growing from one another.

After his experiences in college, Max decided to go to graduate school to study literature written by people of color. He teaches classes at a local community college that look at issues of identity and resistance within oppressive systems. Many of his students cite his classes as having the most impact on their learning and leadership development.

Racial Identity Development Is Different for Different People

Why are these stories important? These characters are made up, but they demonstrate what racial identity development might look like in different people. Granted, these two individuals had a lot of other things in common. Neither had to deal with other parts of their identity that would have been difficult to navigate: neither is gay, both came from economically secure families, neither struggled with mental illness or other forms of disability, they both grew up in the same white neighborhood that had good schools and abundant resources, and both of their families had been living in the United States for several generations and were not viewed as "foreigners." Racial identity development does not just take place in a vacuum—it is related to a number of other factors that make persons who they are. How a person views his or her racial identity is impacted by these other factors as well.

In fact, any of these factors can increase the challenge exponentially.

In the television drama series *When We Rise,*[3] documenting the gay liberation movement and based on real persons, one of the characters is a black man named Ken. Over the course of the movement, we see Ken's attempts to bring awareness of the crisis of the AIDS epidemic to the black community. Ken appears before a city council board and speaks about the need to address the problem of AIDS in the black community. One of the members of the council looks at Ken and tells him: "This is a gay problem. No *real* black men are gay."

Ken takes a deep breath, and then tells the room that he is standing there as a proud black gay man, and that he served his country through several tours during Vietnam in the Navy, and he is proud of who he is. He urges the council to pay attention to this plague killing men, women, and children by acknowledging the presence of gay members of the black community. The council member turns away from Ken and calls on the next presenter.

This scene depicts a real struggle for members of communities of color in which being LGBTQ means you have to pick your community. Ken faced racism from the gay community in San Francisco, and he faced homophobia from the black community. Most of the people Ken associated with were white people and people of color who accepted his sexual orientation and the color of his skin, often because they were also members of the gay community. He gets involved with a church called "City of Refuge" that welcomes persons of different sexual orientations and gender identities, and also provides a food bank and soup kitchen for the local community.

At one point, a minister of Ken's church, a black trans-woman, is killed in a car crash. The brother and mother of the woman come for the funeral, and Ken meets them to tell them about her and what a lovely person she was. The brother reacts angrily to Ken, telling him not to call his brother "a her" and that it was disrespectful to their mother. Ken has to walk away and find

3   *When We Rise.* Created by Dustin Lance Black. ABC Studios, 2017. Miniseries available online.

support from a more conservative white pastor to help convince the woman's brother and mother to honor the woman's identity and the community with which she served in ministry.

For Ken, racial identity development looked different than it would have for someone such as Ashley. He grew up in an earlier era, serving in the Navy during Vietnam, facing racism in the military and silence regarding sexual orientation. Over the course of his life, he witnessed the plague of the AIDS epidemic and the passage of the Defense of Marriage Act and "Don't Ask, Don't Tell." He also lived through the Supreme Court decision that made it possible for LGBTQ persons to get married in every state across the country. His racial identity was different not only because of the era in which he grew up, but also because of the community that most significantly impacted his identity. Being gay for Ken meant he was marginalized from the black community. At the same time, being gay did not spare him from racism in the gay community.

Similarly, a white person who has other aspects of their identity emerge in a significant way will also have different experiences of being white. As I will share in a later story, a white person who grows up in poverty will have a different experience of race than Max. Similarly, a white woman who has a mental illness or who experiences domestic violence will also experience race differently. This is not to suggest that these other experiences related to one's identity will make it easier to see one's race as significant; in fact, it could be that these other aspects make it harder for a person to build connections across races for solidarity. Sometimes people feel the need to focus on only one issue, so they resist feeling pulled to support other causes.

The following are only some of the differences that can impact how you as an individual experience racial identity: age, where you grew up, current neighborhood and places you've lived, gender, sexual orientation, class, education level, working environment, the ideas and values expressed by your parents, if you have a physical or mental disability, or if you are discriminated against because of your religious tradition, nationality, or immigration status. Black persons from Puerto Rico or Cameroon will have different experiences and understandings of being "black" than a black person born and raised in New York City or a small town in Texas. Similarly, imagine being a white person who has immigrated from Serbia or is a Jewish descendant of Holocaust survivors and how very different your understanding would be of what it means to be white, compared to a white Christian born and raised in Phoenix or Milwaukee.

Noting the ways that racial identity development can be different for individuals, what important lessons can these stories of Ashley and Max and the stages they demonstrate help us to learn? Simply knowing the progressive stages of racial identity development can help us understand what stage we are currently in, which one we've recently emerged from, and which stages we have to look forward to in our movement toward racial justice. If we can recognize they have common markers and experiences, we can better listen to our feelings and our experiences, and determine how we can best move forward in working for justice for all. Ken's idea of working for justice meant accepting his black identity and his gay identity and being proud of both. Because race has been such a significant category in the history of discrimination and division in this country, it is a category we need to attend to in order to address the continuing injustice of racism. Racism is not the only form of oppression that impacts persons with intersecting identities, but neither can we ignore race if we're to work for justice in these other areas as well. They are all connected.

Also, it is important to notice stages such as the "reintegration" stage of white racial identity, when we may be projecting negative feelings onto someone else. When we find ourselves becoming angry or feeling defensive, we need to pay attention to what those feelings are. We do not need to deny them, but we can sit with them before we act on them. Letting yourself become more aware of your feelings can help you stay engaged and move forward, rather than projecting your emotions onto persons around you by feeling negatively toward them.

Questions for Reflection and Discussion:

Before moving on to the next chapter, take a moment here to check in with yourself. Take a deep breath. What thoughts and feelings did these stories of racial identity development bring up for you? Write them down in your journal. Circle the feelings that are the strongest for you. Maybe you are experiencing anxiety or resentment, sadness or irritation. Perhaps reading this chapter made you nervous and stressed out or left you feeling guilty at times. I have noticed myself feeling skeptical at times, wondering whether this theory is accurate or helpful. If you have any of these feelings, even doubt or suspicion or any other emotion, write it down. Spend a moment looking at your list, then cover the words you have written, and see if you can name all those feelings and where they come from. Say a prayer over those words and feelings. Ask God to help you honor what you are experiencing and help you experience peace. Thank God for already knowing your heart before you knew yourself.

Afterward, look back over the stages of racial identity development. Turn to the elements you found most helpful. Are there any you felt a strong connection to? Did you find yourself nodding at a particular place? Where do you find you've grown within these stages? What kind of experiences have brought you to where you are now? Have you ever been angry with someone, only to eventually realize that your feelings toward them were outward signs of what was going on inside of you? When are you most likely to feel negatively about someone? What can you do to remind yourself next time to first sit with your emotions and investigate why you may be feeling the way you do? Share with another person your discoveries and decisions, naming the stages of racial identity development that best describe your own life experiences.

Chapter 4

LISTENING TO DIFFERENT STORIES ABOUT RACE

Stories are important for helping us to understand our own experiences and the experiences of others. Hearing stories helps us to connect, to build a sense of community, and to learn from one another. Stories have a way of bringing us together. In this chapter, I share several stories that have been told to me that have helped me gain a better understanding of the different experiences people have living with white skin than if they are not white. These stories have created an opening, even if only a glimpse, into the life of another person's experience.

White Criminals

I was teaching a class to doctor of ministry students on the role of stories, and part of the class involved learning how to tell our own personal stories. I gave the students a prompt and allowed them to think about how they would tell their stories, and then we began sharing our stories with one another. The prompt was this: tell me a story about the first time, or one of the first times, you broke the law.

The students were full of energy, thinking about their stories and then crafting them to share. During the delivery time of the exercise, the room was contagious with laughter. One student told the story of being at a church camp in middle school and being committed to making new friends, which meant that he bravely went up to a group of the cool kids and asked if he could hang out with them. The cool kids said yes, but that meant that he was walking into a situation in which the kids were sharing a tub of chewing tobacco. Instead of saying "no," he went along and took a chunk, but in order to avoid getting caught, he swallowed it. Not a minute too soon, because a camp counselor immediately walked in on the boys, and saw the tobacco stuck in the braces of most of the other boys. The student telling the story, however, had a clean mouth, so he avoided getting in trouble and being sent home. But as the other boys were being picked up from church camp by angry parents, the student who had been seen as innocent spent a terrible night getting sick from swallowing that tobacco!

Another student was hesitant to share any story about breaking the law, because she viewed herself as a rule-follower. She asked when I told her the prompt: "Does it have to be breaking the law? Could it be something like speeding?" (Apparently, as a rule-follower, she felt she could justify speeding from time to time). So I said, "Sure." When she shared her story, she told us about the first time she was given a speeding ticket. She was driving on a street where the speed limit was posted at a much slower speed than she thought was necessary. She had told herself there was no good reason for the speed limit to be so slow, so she didn't bother slowing down when she saw a police car on a side road. She saw the police car, and while she immediately knew she was speeding, she told herself: "If I slow down, then *he* will know that *I* knew I was speeding." So she kept going at the speed she had been driving. Well, the sirens went off and the red-and-blue lights flashed behind her and she was pulled over. She was surprised and taken aback by how upsetting this was for her. She was crying by the time the policeman walked up to her car. The officer came over to her window and said: "I *know* you saw me. If you had just slowed down, I wouldn't have had to pull you over."

A third student shared about a time when she was growing up in a rural area in the Midwest when she stole a pack of gum from the town convenience store. She set up the story by talking about the rolling hills in the area, how the few families that lived in the area all knew one another, and how everyone looked after one another. These families were mostly poor, but they were able to get by. She couldn't remember why it was that one day when going into the town store that she looked around, reached down and pocketed a pack of gum.

She left the store and found herself running all the way home. She felt the shame of what she had done welling up inside of her. Later, she returned to the store, went in quickly and left money on the counter without saying what she had done. This memory had come back to her recently when she was shopping in an upscale boutique in her New Jersey town. The store owner had followed her as she made her way to the back of the store holding onto a box of stationary. She had a feeling the store owner was watching her, but she told herself there were other reasons he was there. But the feeling of being assumed to be a shoplifter ruffled her feathers. She was no shoplifter! But then, this old memory of her childhood came back to haunt her, and she was filled with shame—she *had* been a shoplifter at one time.

A fourth student who was originally from Scotland shared a story about being caught riding her bike on a pedestrian walkway at her college. She had been late for class, so even though she knew it was against the school rules to ride her bike on the pedestrian walkways, she knew it was the fastest way to class. But as she rounded a bend, up ahead stood a campus police officer. She knew she was caught. She knew she would have to stop. But the question she asked herself was, "Do I stop *in front* of the police officer? Or do I stop my bike *just after* I've rolled over his foot?" She chose the latter.

As we listened to these stories, the group of us laughed and delighted in the transgressions that these ministers were confessing. The moment felt lighthearted and sweet. All of the students seemed to enjoy this poignant moment of sharing in these stories with one another.

A few days later, I was with a group of other religion scholars at a retreat. We were all professors at seminaries and theological schools across the country, and we had gathered for a weekend at the beach as part of a teaching cohort sponsored by the Wabash Center for Teaching and Learning Religion. Over the time we had spent with one another, this group of scholars had come to know one another. We felt like friends.

On the last night of the retreat, we had a bonfire at the beach. We were all seated in beach chairs bundled up against the chilly night air around the fire. At a moment when the conversation had a died down, I decided it might be fun to see how this group would respond to the same prompt that I had asked from my doctor of ministry students. So I asked the group: "Can we share stories with each other? I feel like campfires are good places for storytelling. What about telling stories about the first time you broke the law?" I thought that, since the previous group of people who had answered this prompt had seemed so engaged by telling these stories, a group of seminary professors would have a similar attitude.

A woman to my right started: "Well, I don't know if I can tell you a story about the first time I actually *broke* the law. But I can tell you a story about the first time that someone *accused* me of breaking the law!" The tone in her voice was not one of delight, but of pain. She told us about going shopping with a friend. They had visited one shop already where the storyteller had bought something. When they went to the next store, the woman telling the story waited up front for her friend while the friend went around to pick out what she needed there.

The storyteller said that a security guard came up to her and asked roughly: "Are you trying to steal something?"

She said, "No, officer, I was just waiting here for my friend."

"What's in your bag?" he asked.

"Just what I bought at another store, sir," and she showed him the contents of her bag.

She was terrified and felt guilty, worried that she had done something wrong. And it took her a while to realize: she *had* done nothing wrong. She was simply waiting for her friend. But her friend was white, and she was black. That was the first of many experiences she had like that. Around the campfire, we all shared a moment of silence, and the sharing of stories ended there.

In that moment of hearing my colleague's story, I realized how different these two experiences of sharing stories were, and I noticed what I have till now left unmentioned about the activity with the students: the group of doctor of ministry students were all white, and my group of faculty colleagues consisted mostly of people of color—two different groups of people, two different sets of experiences. For the first group, telling about a story when they broke the law felt a little exciting, a little rebellious, coming from people who are ministers, who are assumed to be rule-followers. But being white, these students had never experienced someone else assuming they were criminals. They were usually presumed innocent. On the other hand, my colleague who was black did not convey the feeling that telling stories about breaking the law was exciting or rebellious. The prompt brought up painful memories of times when she was assumed to be a criminal simply because she was black. She shared one of her earliest memories of being accused of breaking the law, an accusation that happened many more times after that.

Have you ever broken the law? If you were invited by someone else to share your earliest memory of breaking the law, what feelings would emerge for you? Would you feel rebellious and share a story that made people laugh? Or would you feel upset, remembering when others wrongly accused you of breaking the law, feeling that others saw you as a criminal when you were innocent? What do these kinds of stories have to do with your experience of race?

I think back on the history of race in the United States, and I notice how, throughout our country's history, people of color have been labeled lawbreakers for doing things that should have been their right to do. Enslaved persons escaping for their freedom: this was against the law. Drinking from a water fountain that white people used: this was against the law. Sitting in the front of the bus: this was against the law. Wanting to marry a white person: this was against the law. And from the story my colleague shared, apparently just standing in a store made her a suspect of breaking the law.

As I write this, my heart grows heavy, thinking about the ways the law has treated white people differently than people of color. It makes me deeply sad. I feel the weight of injustice. And I think about the stories of persons who have been unjustly accused, imprisoned, and even put to death for crimes they did not commit.

The psalmist writes words that lament this, crying out, "How long, O LORD? Will you forget me forever? / How long will you hide your face from me?" (Ps. 13:1).

The Truth and Reconciliation Oral History Project

On February 18, 2017, a group of 80 students from across the state of Texas gathered at Texas Southern University in Houston to conduct interviews. These interviews were part of a Truth and Reconciliation Oral History Project. I and eight other faculty members from the represented schools served as advisors. The project director and founder, Steve Miller, envisioned this project as a way of helping persons who had experienced racial discrimination to be able to tell their stories, both for their own benefit and for the benefit of others who would learn about their experiences. From Miller's past work with persons who had experienced discrimination, he found that the telling of the story was a major component of the person's healing, more than a legal action or some form of restitution. The telling of the story to someone else who was really listening, someone who could say, "I hear you," was itself a powerful source of healing.

Miller recruited faculty support from several Historically Black Colleges and Universities (HBCUs) in Texas, as well as the institution where I teach, Austin Presbyterian Theological Seminary, because he earned his masters of divinity from our school. He also recruited faculty from Baylor University's Institute for Oral History and scholars from New York who were also interested in stories for understanding history and social justice movements. Miller worked for months to raise funds to support students and faculty from the participating institutions traveling to Houston, staying overnight, and spending a whole day interviewing persons who volunteered to share their stories. The sheer effort behind this one-day event impressed me.

Three students from Austin Seminary joined me in traveling to Houston for the event. My students were all white, so they worked with students from other institutions to conduct the interviews in order to create a more inviting environment for the interviewees. We assumed that persons who were there to share their stories about racial discrimination, most likely from white people, would feel uncomfortable being interviewed by three white students. Each student was paired up with a student from one of the HBCUs, and the two students would together take turns acting as interviewer and operating the recording equipment.

The day of the event came, and everything was ready. The rooms were reserved for all of the participating students and scholars at the hotel and at the Texas Southern Law School where the interviews would be conducted. Rooms were designated for hospitality where snacks and drinks were available for persons getting interviewed, as well as for grief and counseling in case someone wanted to speak with a counselor after sharing their story. The planning and arrangement of these spaces communicated to persons who came: "This is nurturing space, and we are grateful that you are sharing your story with us today."

As a faculty advisor, I was not assigned an interview team, but instead worked to make sure the interviewers had what they needed. At one point, I went out to buy 30 boxes of tissues for the interview rooms. As the day went on, I was hoping that I would be able to sit in and listen to one of the interviews. All of these stories would be eventually transcribed and shared more broadly, but I wanted to be there in the moment with persons who were sharing this gift with us.

Eventually, I got my chance. Due to shortages of interviewers, I was able to interview a few people who came in late in the day—among them, Texas State House Representative Jarvis Johnson.

Meeting Jarvis Johnson

Johnson walked into the Law School building accompanied by a woman whom I had met at a previous gathering of advisors and planners for this event; she worked at a local radio station in their advertising department. She and her two children came in with Mr. Johnson, and she spoke with the receptionist: "Mr. Johnson would like to tell his story." He looked reluctant. Dressed in an elegant suit and a handsome tie, he appeared too busy to be able to give up some of his time to sit down and tell a story. Steve Miller, the event organizer, greeted him warmly and led him up to the briefing room, the first step in the process—where the person getting interviewed learns about the process and what to expect. Miller led him back downstairs afterward and asked, "Who is going to interview Mr. Johnson? Persons should be lining up to do this job." I was the only person within close range as he made this statement, so I raised both hands.

"I would love to. Can I?"

Steve led Mr. Johnson and me into a lecture hall, so that others could join in and watch the interview. I was nervous. First, because I knew I was interviewing a state official. Second, because everyone would be watching. And third, because I felt like I should know more about Mr. Johnson because he was a state official, but I knew nothing about him and felt embarrassed for my ignorance. So the interview began with a few broad questions about his early life and how he got into politics.

I asked, "What journey did you take to get where you are now as a state representative? How did that journey unfold?"

> "I was a drug baby. [pause] Growing up, my mother drug me everywhere I needed to be. She would constantly take me and expose me to everything—every time I didn't want to go, she still took me to all the meetings. My mother was involved in politics; she used to work for the late Mickey Leland. So my introduction to politics was licking stamps and envelopes. And a lot of block walking."

It took me a second to catch his play-on words, that his mother had brought him to events where he was exposed to political action, not that he was an actual "drug baby." When I later learned about the Fifth Ward of Houston, the neighborhood in which he grew up, I realized the poignancy of this pun. The Fifth Ward is an area stricken with poverty, predominantly black—where drugs were indeed part of the challenges of the neighborhood. But drugs were not part of his upbringing; instead, his mother raised him on trying to make a difference.

The interview proceeded with questions and answers that sounded like a political interview, with me asking him questions about how he was currently trying to make a difference, and how he felt the new administration would impact his constituency, and so on. These questions could be asked by a news reporter and relayed in a political ad. But then I started to ask questions that drew out the nonofficial story.

"Have you every experienced a time when you felt like an opportunity was closed to you because of discrimination?"

> "You walk down the street everyday as a black man, so you know that… [stops in mid-sentence and starts anew]. But I ignore that kind of stuff. I think I mentioned to you before that I've ignored racism. I've never let it get into me. But I've experienced it everyday, just as much as black men everyday have to experience racism. I don't think that doors were closed to me, but I've been mentally trained, if you will. Whenever I see a police officer, I don't get nervous. I get scared. Literally. Get scared. And most people wouldn't even understand that. And it's not just me alone, but you're talking about black men all across this country. Literally. Get scared. So then you get angry. And I've experienced those types of situations a number of times, and I think a very unfair number of times that I've had to experience those types of things."

"Could you tell me about one of those times?"

> "Well, recently, I guess it was a few years ago, in 2014. I was pulled over for what they said was speeding. I pulled over. I pulled into a well-lit gas station. And a police officer got out of the car, took two steps outside from his car, pulled his gun, and walked to my door. When my window was down, he put the gun to my face, and asked 'What the f*** was [I] doing?!'"

[Pause].

> He continued, reliving the experience, going back between his remarks and the officer's: "I'm sorry. I don't know what you are talking about. What do you mean what am I doing?' 'Didn't you see my siren?'

'Yeah, and I pulled over.' But I didn't pull over to his liking, I guess. I didn't pull over fast enough.

"Now, from the time at which he put his siren on and the time at which I stopped—I had to go back and measure it later—it was 216 yards. 216 yards. From the time at which he could've put his lights on and the time at which I stopped. Now, he said I was going 50 miles an hour in a 35, so if I was even going 50, how fast does it take a car to go 216 yards? If you're going 50 miles an hour, you tell me I didn't stop fast enough for you? And so that was your right—and so from there, he puts the gun to my face and then he tells me to get out of the car, so I step out of the car.

"And he pushes me against the car and tells me to put my hands up on the car. Now, my back is to my car, and I can't put my hands up on the car so I literally stuck my hands on the car like that [showing his hands low behind his back facing against an invisible car]. He thought I was being funny.

"I don't know what to do. I get nervous; I don't know what to do right now.

"Eventually, another police officer came over. Now that police officer grabbed me; one held my arms, the other put handcuffs on me. They patted me down, took all of the things that were in my pockets and set them on my car seat, and then walked me over and put me in the back of his car where I had to sit for the next 35 minutes.

"And then other officers came. Other officers started coming, it was about 9 of them. They got my ID. They took it to the officer while the others searched my car. So from there, obviously I don't think they knew who I was at the time, and I'm not saying I wasn't anybody, but they didn't know who I was. It was a constable and the Houston police department was there as well. So when they ran my ID, the Houston police department just left—all 9 officers, just gone. So I was there with him, and I'm sitting in the back of the car for 35 minutes. He then let me out, took my handcuffs off, and handed me back my license and said, 'You're free to go.' I don't understand what I was pulled over for in the first place!

"He did give me a ticket for speeding. So at the end of the day, I got *handcuffed,* I got a *gun* put to my face, and I got thrown in the back seat of the car. For *speeding.*"

As he spoke, I noticed the change that came over him. Though dressed in a suit and tie, a man who stood over six feet tall with a deep voice carrying all the authority of being an elected state official, here he sounded like a frightened child by an experience that was more than humiliating; it was terrifying. Looking at Mr. Johnson walk into a room, it is hard to imagine anything intimidating him. But hearing his story, I recognized that no amount of political power or success could prevent this black man from feeling as if none of that mattered when it came to an encounter with a police officer with a gun. Too many news stories have played that scene out with terrible and deadly results.

He continued: "So when I'm free to go, I asked him where were all my belongings? And he said, 'They're in your console,' and I said, 'Sir, why did you go inside my console? Once you took all my money, my keys, and my wallet out of my pocket, you put it on the seat.' ...He said 'Dude, I told you...' and I said, 'My name is not Dude. It is either Jarvis or Mr. Johnson.' The other officer then started walking my way, saying 'You need to calm down,' and he grabbed for his gun. He says, 'You need to calm down.' And as calm as I'm talking to you was as calm as I was talking to him.

"So, then I walk to my car, and the officers walked to my car. And they both stood at my car. For another 25 minutes.

"Now I never left, and I wasn't going to leave. Because typically when you get a ticket, the officer writes you a ticket, says you're free to go, and then the officer typically leaves. Well that officer didn't leave. He just stood there.

"So I thought, I'm not going anywhere, let me go and get some gas. I walked into the store. And the officer walks into the store. I walked out of the store, the officer walked out of the store. As I was getting gas and letting the pump by itself, I thought, 'I wonder if they have cameras here.' So I walk back into the store, and the officer walks back into the store. So that went on.

"Until finally I called for a sergeant to come out. And the sergeant got there, and from there, I felt comfortable. After he sent them on their way, and then I went on my way.

"That was the first time in my life that I've ever been scared for my life. And I'm typically not a scared person. And I've had incidents like that since then. Now I've lived in what they consider some of the roughest parts of Houston. I grew up in 5th Ward.

"I've never had a gun pulled on me by anybody, but by law enforcement. On three different occasions. That was just the most recent. On three different occasions. And again, I don't have a criminal history. I've never been arrested. I've never been jailed. But those are the situations that I've had to deal with, and that's the kind of situation that goes on all across this country."

I then asked, "You mentioned earlier that the scared feeling turns to anger. You feel scared, and then you feel angry. In what ways do you feel your anger has helped you focus some of your political work?"

Laughing, he tells me: "My anger has never helped me in anyway, so I try not to use my anger at all."

And then, taking a more serious tone: "But I thank God it did happen. Because it does happen so often. And you feel so *powerless*. When you ask the question why was I *handcuffed?* Why was I *frisked?* Why was I *thrown in the back of the police car?* For no justifiable reason for you to do it? We don't do that to citizens just because you gave me a speeding ticket. You just did it because you felt like it.

"Officers you've heard over the last few years who've shot black men, the first things they've said is they feared for their life. How did you fear for your life while he was running *away* from you? How did you fear for your life when he didn't even have a *weapon* on him? How did you fear for your life when *you* actually *provoked* the situation? You were supposed to come in and calm the situation down and you actually incite it?

"You get confused. Could I have gotten shot because I disobeyed his order to put my hands against the car? You're pushing me up against my own car with my back against the car. When I try to put my hands on the car you get frustrated and feel insulted and think I'm being funny. What do I do? So we have to create laws.

"I support law enforcement. I support them for the time in which I don't have to call them. But in every group there's a bad apple. A bad apple can make it bad for the entire population. And we need to set laws that give punitive consequences for police officers. Who would shoot an individual and then say 'I feared for my life.'

"Tamir Rice—you drove up within feet of him. Why didn't you stay in your car, where you were protected? If you really thought he had a gun? Why didn't you stand away and use your megaphone and say, 'Please, sir. You have a gun? Put it down. Put it down, please.' Why didn't you do that? Why did you drive into that situation, and shoot him because you thought he had a gun?

"The other day I saw a cop being chased by an individual. He was shooting at the cop. And they took him *alive*. Wow. *That's* how you are supposed to deal with situations. A guy ran into a gas station and blew everything up, and he was going crazy, and he attacked the cop. The cop retreated, and he kept attacking the cop. They were able to take him alive. Of course, both of those individuals were white.

"I don't need to provoke an officer for him to shoot me. Simply my skin color. Why? I don't know. I don't know.

"But that's what I deal with, that's what my son deals with. And that's what I'm afraid of in this country today.

"The fact that, at any given time, a police officer can roll up next to me, shoot me, and then there is no consequence to his action. None.

"And we've seen it over and over and over again.

"How do you *choke* Eric Garner because he was selling *cigarettes* on the street? Was that justification for having those many officers *choking* him?

"Those stories go on and on. You've heard all the stories. And yet each time, *each time*, they've been exonerated.

"And had it not simply been in today's society for video...

"The gentleman [Philando Castile] who gets pulled over and the officer says 'let me see your driver's license.' And the guy turns to get his driver's license. And the cop shoots him! And he asks, 'Why did you shoot me?' 'Because I thought you were going for your gun,' 'But you told me to get my driver's license!' How did he pose a threat?

"And these stories go on. And it becomes frustrating when you hear those people being exonerated. So yes, it happens. And I have to use my experience to craft legislation that will make sure that this does not happen.

"Officers have one of the most dangerous jobs. We send our soldiers off to war, and they come back with PTSD. But our police officers see battle every single day, and there is never a time when the police are required to get mental checks. There is no time when they have to be psychologically evaluated. To be an officer, you just get a credit check.

"So I have to craft legislation based on my experiences. So hopefully, my son doesn't have to go through this, or anybody's son have to go through this."

Hearing this story, I couldn't help but feel frightened myself. I could imagine the scene in my mind, and I had all the other images of police confrontations with black men in which the men have ended up dead. I saw this man sitting in front of me and thought: *He could have been shot. He could have been killed.* And no amount of fame or money or political influence would have saved him. He is a black man, and as long as black men continue to be seen as criminals, he will continue to risk his life in situations like a traffic stop or a speeding ticket. He is assumed already to be guilty, even though he has been working his entire career to improve the living conditions of Houston's poor black population. Where is the justice?

If you are reading this as a white person, have you ever been pulled over by the police for speeding? What was your experience like? Were you worried about your physical safety? Did an officer ever point at gun at you? Have you ever been handcuffed and put in the back of a police car? What would you be feeling if you were in Mr. Johnson's shoes in that moment? Mr. Johnson said that this was not the only experience he has had like this one, only the most recent. What if this kind of experience happened to you more than once? What if you were pulled over many times and had an experience like this? If you are meeting with a small group to discuss these chapters, take time to share your reactions to hearing about Mr. Johnson's experience.

Hearing Guwayne

Guwayne was sitting at a table by himself in the cafeteria. We were on a lunch break from conducting interviews for the Oral History Project. Wanting to make friends and get to know people, I asked if I could join him. He said I could, so I put down my tray of meatloaf and collards and hung my purse on the back of the seat. Then, I went looking for silverware. I came back and sat down, and we both enjoyed our lunches for a few moments before I began asking questions.

"So what school are you with?" I asked.

"Wiley College," he said.

"And where are you from originally?"

"The same area."

"The area around Wiley?"

"Yeah."

He was dressed sharply in a crisp white button down and a tie. His skin was the color of milk chocolate, and he had a short beard lining his jaw. His cheeks looked worn, like the result of scarring, either through injury or adolescent acne. I had initially assumed he was the same age as most of the kids coming from the colleges and universities—between 19 and 22. But now, I could see he was older.

I asked him how the interviews were going, and he said pretty well. Then he added, "But I've seen everything already, so there's nothing that surprises me." I asked what he meant.

"I've been in the state penitentiary, and they keep you separated by race. You don't know how bad racism can get until you've been in the pen." Suddenly aware that I was sitting with a former inmate, I thought back to having left my purse at my seat and worried whether he had been tempted to steal it. I immediately felt embarrassed for allowing that thought to even cross my mind. I tried to focus on what he was sharing with me.

"What do you mean—what was it like?" I asked.

"They don't even let you room with a person from another race. Blacks have to room with blacks, whites with whites, Mexicans with Mexicans. And everyone sticks to their own race. Like, if someone from your race starts a riot, you got to join in too, even if you don't agree with the guy who started it. Because, if you don't help him now, no one is going to help you when you need it. And you've got guys walking around with knives, and you don't have anything, and the guards are on the side of some guys and will sneak in weapons for them. So you need people to have your back.

"I'm almost 40 years old, and all these younger kids with us here—they haven't seen anything. They don't know how lucky they have it. I'm just glad I'm on the other side, that I'm back in school. That my life has changed."

"So how did you change? What led you to getting out and doing something different?"

"This was my third time in the penitentiary. Right before I went in, my son was born, and then my grandmother died. I knew I had to do something different. I couldn't just grow old in there. I needed to get out and make something of myself."

"What got you in there?"

"Drugs. I was a hustler. I was in the pen twice before I was 25. Then a third time before I was 30. That last time, they picked me up because they were looking for some other guy. They wanted me to snitch him out, but I wouldn't do it. So they got me instead. It's not like I was innocent; I had been selling drugs too, so I couldn't really fight it. I got 15 years, served nine."

"You got 15 years for selling drugs? That seems like a long time! I mean, there's a lot of other people doing a lot of bad things who don't get put in prison for that long."

"I know. And they're making a lot of money off of us. It doesn't cost but 50 cents to feed us every day in the pen—we make our own clothes, we grow our own food, we slaughter our own animals. But the people running the jail get like billions of dollars a year just for keeping us in prison. It's not right. That's why I want to go back and work in the criminal justice system. I want to work with young kids and keep them out of jail."

"Have you read a book by Michelle Alexander, *The New Jim Crow*?" I asked.

"Yeah—I've heard of it—we were discussing it this week in class, actually. But I had to miss it because I'm here. But my friend said she would give me the notes."

Now a felon, Guwayne doesn't have the right to vote. He can't get a good job. He is stuck in poor-paying jobs for the rest of his life. He had told me that he got into selling drugs because that was the only way to make real money in his hometown. He grew up poor, and there were no jobs, no way for people to get ahead, except for selling drugs. The people selling drugs had the flashy cars, and made it look good. But now he has had to pay for it with years of his life in prison, missing the first nine years of his son's life. He has deep regrets, and yet he also knows he has been treated unfairly.

The New Jim Crow

Michelle Alexander wrote a book entitled *The New Jim Crow: Mass Incarceration in the Age of Colorblindness*. The book talks about mass incarceration as a new form of "Jim Crow" laws that make it legal for persons to discriminate against people of color. Mass incarceration refers to the higher rates of imprisoning black and brown people than white people and unequal patterns of sentencing.

The Netflix documentary *13th* is about the 13th amendment, the constitutional insertion that abolished slavery, but that also provided a loophole: "Neither slavery nor involuntary servitude, *except as a punishment for crime*…shall exist within the United States…" This loophole, "except as a punishment for crime," meant a drastic rise in the number of prisons directly after the end of slavery, when African Americans who were now free were arrested on charges such as loitering or trespassing, and sentenced to jail. Once in jail, they were forced to work like slaves in some of the same fields where African Americans had worked previously as slaves. This legacy has continued, with blacks being more likely to be stopped by the police, arrested, and put in jail than their white counterparts. And once in jail, they lose many of their basic rights. Persons can be labeled a "felon" for minor drug charges, and, once they are felons, they lose the right to vote. In some states, that right is permanently revoked. Other consequences may include losing Section 8 or affordable housing eligibility, and some states ban persons convicted of drug felonies from receiving food stamps or nutritional assistance. They are often discriminated against when looking for work.

Thinking about Guwayne, I wonder how many other black men have had their lives snuffed out through cycles of poverty and discriminatory drug laws. If white people were caught and imprisoned for doing and selling drugs at the same rate as black people, the prisons would be considerably more overcrowded than they are now. But that is not the case. White people who are wealthy can afford better lawyers and can get away with doing or selling drugs because the areas where they live are less frequented by police. They do not have drug raids. The kind of drugs that whites consume are not as criminalized as crack cocaine.

Many white people are afraid of black people. White people associate blacks with crime. But what kind of crime makes us most afraid? If it is violent crime, then we should be more afraid of other white people, since white men have been responsible for most of the mass shootings that have taken place across our country (Columbine, Newtown, the movie theater in Colorado, Charleston, Las Vegas, etc.). If it is the fear of being robbed, then we should again be more afraid of white men, because of the amount of money that white men have stolen through huge scandals—the Houston Enron executives, Bernie Madoff's investment scandal and other Ponzi schemes named after white men, the Lehmann Brothers bail out, the sub-prime mortgage fiasco. Politicians who are paid by taxpayers to serve the public interest can use taxpayer money (in effect, stealing from the public) to protect corporate interests instead. These are the thieves who are responsible for gutting our retirement accounts, for shutting down factories and sending jobs overseas, for valuing the bottom line over human lives. So why aren't white people afraid of these other white people?

Another reason white people are afraid of black people is that they fear the anger that black people have toward whites. White people, either consciously or unconsciously, are aware of the anger that a group of people may have toward them because of the centuries of slavery and discrimination that white people have enacted against black people. Awareness of the potential anger that could be directed against us makes us afraid. We are afraid of being punished, of others seeking retribution for past wrongs. Either rationally or irrationally, we fear recompense for the past cruelty and injustice white people have perpetuated against others.

So we maintain segregation. We keep separate neighborhoods, we hire people who look like us, or only the people of color who are very friendly and easy to work with and who never complain or rock the boat. If white people see a black person in their neighborhood, they call the police and report a "suspicious person." This fear of persons of color continues the cycle of racial discrimination, because white people are more likely to judge negatively those whom they fear. White people may consciously acknowledge the injustice of racial discrimination, but as long as they are afraid of black people or other people of color, they will continue to act in ways that further racial discrimination.

"Perfect love casts out fear." This scripture verse from 1 John 4:18 gives an example of what we can do with our fear. We can turn it into love. Focusing on our fear, we can meditate on the person or persons to whom our fears are directed, and imagine ourselves loving them instead. The "perfect love" that we are called to live out is not something that we on our own can achieve, but through prayer and practice we can work toward greater love for others.

Sometimes working toward greater loves means first noticing when we are afraid. A friend of mine, who is an immigrant from India, relayed an experience of getting in a taxi leaving the airport in Los Angeles. She and the driver both had dark brown skin, and they both had accents. Starting up small talk, she asked where he was from. He answered: Pakistan. As soon as she learned this, fear consumed her. Should she get out of the cab? Could she escape if he attacked her? Her palms began to sweat and her heart raced. She assumed he would be a terrorist. But as her rational mind caught up with her, she told herself: *Of course he is not a terrorist!*

Why am I so afraid? There is nothing to fear in this situation. She had grown up in India being taught to fear Pakistanis, and she realized this was the first time she had ever actually met someone from Pakistan.

We are taught to fear. Noticing fear and talking ourselves out of that fear is essential if we are to overcome the biases we were once taught.

Questions for Reflection and Discussion:

If you have a journal you are writing in, take a moment to write down the feelings you experienced reading these stories. Can you remember a time when you felt afraid of someone else because of what you had been taught? Were you able to talk yourself out of that fear? Have you ever felt like someone was afraid of you for no reason? Or has someone acted like they thought you were suspicious?

Reflect on how it feels to hear the different stories told by white people, and then a black woman, in response to the prompt: "When was the first time you broke the law?" For me, I felt embarrassed and sad. For my friend to have experienced the suspicion that she had broken the law multiple times throughout her life simply because of the color of her skin, I felt so oblivious to have asked the question in the first place. I realized how the question already came out of my white experience of being presumed innocent: when no one suspects you, the feeling of doing something bad can sometimes feel "good," or at least humorous. But for my friend who had never had the luxury of being presumed innocent, there were no good feelings associated with breaking any kind of law.

What about the stories of Texas State Representative Jarvis Johnson? What emotions did this story bring up for you? When I was listening to Mr. Johnson, I could feel his fear. I felt scared myself listening to his experience. I also felt angry that this experience happened to him, and this was not an isolated event for him or anyone else who looks like him. Black families regularly have to give their children "the talk" to learn how to respond in case a police officer pulls them over, what to say and do so as to avoid being shot. I have never had to have that conversation with my children. So the feelings I felt when listening to his story were ones of anger and frustrations and sadness. What were your reactions?

What about Guwayne? Have you ever known anyone like Guwayne, who has made some mistakes in life and has had to pay for those mistakes? Does it seem fair to you that Guwayne should spend that much time in jail for drug charges, and be labeled a felon for the rest of his life? What are some ways you think we could do better as a country to help the poor and to rehabilitate those who have been imprisoned? Who benefits from mass incarceration? Spend time reflecting on these questions, and, if you are in small groups, take time to discuss your responses with another person or two.

I realize there's a lot I don't know. Let me alone already. What does this have to do with faith?

Chapter 5

EXPRESSING GRATITUDE

Talking about race and racism means more than understanding how we learn to interpret, and more than individual self-awareness of how one has been racialized within our society and the emotional reactions that come with this process. In addition to attending to our own emotions, we also need a guiding framework for approaching these conversations and how we interact with others as we work for racial justice. This guiding framework is necessary for whites as they enter conversations about race and racism, and I propose *gratitude* as the best framework.

A framework of gratitude may seem counterintuitive. When most people think about conversations on race, they get anxious and fearful. That fear comes from the assumption that there will be conflict, that they will be put into "fight or flight" mode. In political philosophy, there is a term for the conflict between persons from different cultural identities—not only race but also gender and sexual orientation and other forms of identity that have been the basis for discrimination. This phrase is the "struggle for recognition." Such a struggle involves the conflict of one group that feels oppressed by another group, seeking to make their grievances heard. Groups that have been marginalized and silenced must work to gain the attention of those in power, struggling to be recognized and seen as fully human, deserving of respect and equal rights. Several political philosophers have written insightful books that describe this process.[1]

But if those in power always expect a struggle, if they anticipate conflict, it is not likely the powerful group will want to continue the conversation. Most people tend to avoid conflict if possible. So perhaps there is another way we can think about this process, particularly for those of us who hold social power.

Hermeneutic philosopher Paul Ricoeur introduces another way of understanding the word *recognition*.[2] Applied to our discussion, his work can help whites understand difficult conversations in another way. Ricoeur finds that the word *recognition* sometimes refers to gratitude, such as someone being "recognized" for their contributions. Ricoeur suggests that viewing mutual recognition through the lens of gratitude, such as in a gift exchange, helps us anticipate such conversations less in terms of inevitable conflict and antagonism, and instead as opportunities to share gifts with one another and express gratitude. Viewing recognition as gratitude can lead to additional opportunities for these experiences of mutual recognition—gift exchanges that lead to further gratitude, rather than never-ending struggle.

In my work, the idea that gratitude may have a central role to play in our conversations about race and racism has been both controversial and effective. Thinking about gratitude as it relates to racial injustice can be controversial in that it presupposes there is something there to be grateful for, even on the part of those identified as the oppressors. That idea can be very disorienting.

---

1 Axel Honneth, *The Struggle for Recognition*, (Cambridge, Mass.: MIT Press, 1992); Honneth and Nancy Fraser, *Redistribution or Recognition? A Political-Philosophical Exchange* (London, New York: Verso, 2003); and Kelly Oliver, *Witnessing Beyond Recognition* (Minneapolis: Univ. of Minnesota Press, 2001) are all excellent resources for further reading on this.

2 Paul Ricoeur, *The Course of Recognition* (Cambridge, Mass.: Harvard University Press, 2005). Personally, I have found that viewing these conversations through the lens of gratitude—including the idea that I, and others like me, may have gifts to offer in this conversation—has been an inspiring tool for continuing engagement. I am more likely to stay in the conversation.

However, as a white person if I feel I will be receiving a gift through this challenging discussion, and if I anticipate being able to offer gifts, I may participate. If all I anticipate is feeling guilty, then I will consciously or unconsciously resist staying engaged. But if I participate in this conversation because I expect it to lead to gratitude, then I am much more confident and willing to keep talking even amidst the challenging feelings that may come from difficult conversations.

Arguing for a framework of gratitude, and seeing recognition as gratitude, is more than a matter of psychological self-esteem or a strategy for engagement. There are deeper theological reasons that warrant bringing gratitude into these conversations. We do not talk about the ongoing effects of racial discrimination out of guilt or a desire to fulfill some sort of moral obligation. We work on addressing ongoing injustice because of gratitude for the grace we have received from God through Jesus Christ.

The reason behind our conversations about race has to be more than our own human failings—talking about our sin, both past and present, is not enough to call our lives to action. We act out of the belief that we "have been saved through faith, and this is not of [our] own doing; it is the gift of God." (Eph. 2:8-9). The inspiration to work towards greater peace and justice in the world does not come from believing we can save ourselves, but rather that we have been "created in Christ Jesus for good works" (Eph.2:10)—which means that we were *made for this*. The good work of building community with persons from different races who all make up the body of Christ—*this* is what we were created to do. It is the gratitude that comes from our redemption in Christ that moves us to action.

The reason we must continue these conversations is because our gratitude knows no end. We continue to see God's work in the world and in our lives, and we continue to experience the love and grace of God in real and tangible ways. God has not forsaken humanity. Because God has not forsaken us, we are grateful and moved to care and to "work out [our] salvation with fear and trembling" (Phil.2:12) as we live into the gratitude that is our response to God's grace.

If we can talk about race through this deep gratitude that comes from knowing the love of God, then we may be moved to transform the world in which we live. By drawing from the deep well of gratitude that is ours through faith, we can help give strength to those whose feet are faltering in the pursuit of justice, nourishing them with the love of God so that together we can go on with boldness and courage. Gratitude is the source of our action because we have first been loved by God. It is in this experience of gratitude that we turn to others out of a sense of abundance and openness to what they have to offer to the conversation, aware that the love of God unites us with one another even amidst our differences.

Disclaimers about Gratitude

However, a word of caution: gratitude is no gimmick. Gratitude is a natural response to the unmerited grace of a loving God. It is not an obligation or a duty. It is not a feeling that we have gotten something we deserve or sense of self-satisfaction. It is not about feeling good about ourselves for something we have done. Gratitude is not something we command ourselves or others to give. It emerges only as a gift itself, the experience of knowing one is blessed beyond one's control or merit.

When I speak about gratitude in the context of talking about race, there are those who are hesitant about this move toward gratitude. They worry that this move is too quick, that it overrides the call to repentance for whites to turn from feelings of racial superiority. They worry that the move toward recognition as gratitude is a step away from justice by simply reassuring the oppressors that they are loved and forgiven by God. This may be true—this is a valid concern. As in any attempt to preach the gospel of Jesus Christ, there is the danger of offering "cheap grace," as Dietrich Bonhoeffer described it.

Gratitude is risky, and I want to return to Ricoeur to unpack this a bit. He writes that the setting for gratitude is typified by an exchange of gifts, in which one person gives a gift to another out of generosity, and the other person experiences gratitude. The gift receiver may want to give a gift to the giver—not out of obligation, but because of a desire to give. The original giver becomes the gift receiver, and there is another opportunity for gratitude. The two are connected through this exchange of gifts.[3]

But in a gift exchange, there is always the risk that the gift will offend the recipient. Think back to when you tried your best to pick out a gift for a loved one, only to discover the cookbook you thought they'd love made them feel you were giving them dieting advice, or the sweater you bought they felt made them look fat. There is also the risk of one person feeling obligated to give, bound to give or reciprocate a gift. You give a friend an expensive birthday gift, and they feel guilty. Gift exchanges can and do go wrong, which reminds us that gratitude is never a sure thing or something we can predict, plan for or orchestrate. We can try to cultivate it within ourselves, but we cannot control how others respond to the gifts we give in gratitude.

People can also be suspicious of gifts we have to offer. In German, the word *gift* means "poison," and German folklore includes stories of malicious gifts being offered, such as poison put into beer that was gifted to an enemy. The gift of the Trojan horse in Greek mythology is another example of a gift intended to destroy the recipient. Some gifts may not be explicitly intended to harm, but they can be given with strings attached. In churches, members who give generously may also threaten to withhold their pledges unless the pastor makes decisions they agree with. In these gift-giving examples, gratitude would not be the appropriate response. Skepticism and caution are better.

---

3 Ricoeur, *The Course of Recognition*, reflecting on the work of Marcel Mauss, *The Gift: Forms and Functions of Exchange in Archaic Societies*. (Glencoe, Ill.: Free Press, 1954).

Relating this to conversations about race, it is tricky to talk about gratitude in a way that does not miscommunicate. The gratitude to motivate talking about race and to inspire us to get involved in antiracism efforts moves in a one-way direction. This gratitude cannot expect reciprocity, or look for others to be grateful for it. If you join a group of people of color to work for justice, you may be viewed with suspicion. Persons of color will not automatically extend trust to you because of your good intentions. But even if your gifts are viewed with suspicion, stay present and engaged. Accept that others may have a reason for not trusting you right away. Be available and ready to offer your gifts at the best time: when others recognize the need. Gratitude is what motivates *you;* it is not something you expect in return.

I share from my own experience. After completing my PhD dissertation, but before I began teaching, I was invited to be part of a denominational work group on race in the Northeast. I felt honored to be included, but I also expected this group would want me to share some of my research on talking about race with white people. I traveled to New York City from Boston, and when I arrived, I discovered the event was an informal conversation, without any expectations that I share my expertise. I felt irritated, like this was a waste of my time, feeling unrecognized for my gifts. But looking back, I realize I missed an opportunity to learn from the people who assembled there—the group of church leaders who had had different experiences. Had I simply been grateful for being included, rather than expecting others to be grateful for my contribution, I would have opened myself to a better experience. Ironically, any gifts I may have shared were unavailable to me because I made myself unavailable to others through this unspoken expectation. Gratitude as a motivator can only move in one direction, moving us to respond joyfully. If we expect it to come from someone else, gratitude in us morphs into manipulation. To foster gratitude in ourselves, we must be present in the moment, open to the gifts of others.

Meeting Ms. Browning

A couple of people have helped me to think about the complexity of gratitude. One of these people was a woman I interviewed during the Oral History Project (which I described in the previous chapter). She was the first person I interviewed, and the opportunity felt serendipitous. It happened that the last set of interviewers had begun listening to another story and we were down an interview team, so I volunteered.

I was nervous. There were two reasons for this. The first was that the woman's name was Ms. Sherry Browning. Browning is my maiden name. A flash of panic went through my mind: *What if I discover that this woman is somehow related to me? As in, what if I learn that my ancestors enslaved her ancestors?* I didn't feel ready to make such a connection with the sins of the past showing up in the present.

The second reason was her outfit. She had walked in wearing an interesting "costume" of sorts. On one side of her face, her hair was down, and on the other side her hair was pulled up and under a red bandana that looked almost like a big bow. She wore half of an apron, and had one of her pants' legs tucked into her calf-high sock, while the other was left hanging down. She had make-up on only half of her face. She carried around with her a poster that had a few photos on it and hand-written information around the photos. I have a family history of mental illness, and so I worried her eccentric attire might be an expression of mental instability. But I also knew that people are not necessarily mentally ill just because they like to dress eccentrically.

I tried to set aside my nerves and uncertainty and open my heart to whatever she had to share. I also hoped that, if *I* interviewed her, I would not let her outfit distract me, as I worried might be the case with younger student interviewers. I wanted this interview to represent her seriously. I wanted this woman's story to be heard.

Two women accompanied her, and in the interview room they sat behind her a few rows back. At the start of the interview, she remained standing. I asked whether she would like to make herself comfortable, if she would like to sit down. She did. Then, we sat facing each other, and I was able to look into her deep brown eyes. I focused just on her eyes, blocking out the costume.

I started the interview by asking, "Could you share with us a little bit about your background?"

> "Well, my father was in entertainment, and I would go to work with him sometimes—shows with entertainers, mostly musical. He was one of the first blacks to be inducted into Juilliard Conservatory School in New York. He was the guy that Ed Sullivan would call for him to book black entertainment for his show, and Dick Clark.

> "My father, John 'Tootie' Browning—'Tootie' because they would say, 'come out here and toot your horn!' He traveled all over the world, which I didn't like as a kid. Seeing him on television, he'd be in another city on a holiday, and I didn't like that. I'd think 'I wish I had my daddy here with me this Christmas.' As a kid, you don't realize that's how he made his living.

> "But I enjoyed the other part, because the entertainers would have to come by our house to get their sheet music, so it was great meeting Ike and Tina Turner, B.B. King, and people like that.

> "One day I said, 'I need some allowance money! When these people come, can I ask them to get autographs from you all and I keep the money?' So that's how I would make my allowance. When I got older, I got to go to the clubs with them and I would sell their memorabilia."

I asked more about her father, whether he was still living, and this got her talking about the story she was there to tell:

"My father is deceased now, and that's what brings me to this story. Some years ago, he had bought a brand new Continental. I had gotten my chauffeur's license because his aunt and I were going into the limousine service, and we had to get chauffeur's licenses. And my dad had just got this brand new Continental and he let me drive it by *myself*!

"I was going downtown, and when I was driving into the parking lot, I was close to getting in, but not all the way in, and this man comes up and yells, 'You N*****!' And I was like, 'What did I *do*?'

"He just came out of nowhere in his car, saying, 'You took my damn parking space!' And I was going, 'Did he just call me that?' And then he came up and *spit* on my daddy's new car.

"After he passed me by, I moved the car, because I'm saying: 'This is my daddy's brand new car, and he trusted me with his car, and this man may go even further and scratch his car up. So I just parked the car somewhere else and waited a while until I knew where he was going so he wouldn't scratch up my daddy's car. And then he left. And it was devastating to me."

"When you went back home, did you tell this experience to your dad?"

"Oh yeah! I mean, I was devastated! I was in tears. My dad asked if I had a description of the man. He was really mad! But I was just trying to get away from the man—it's not like they had camera phones back then.

"And it was devastating because it was so different from what I'd experienced. My godmother was the richest person in Houston at the time. And I thought back to what she said to me at the time. She said, 'all white people are not bad like that.' But I was thinking, 'He was *horrible*.'

"She told me that not all white people are bad, but I felt like I finally met one! I had never met anybody who wasn't like her, because I was always in her circle of friends, and all of them were really nice to me, just like she was.

"I'm just glad nothing happened to my daddy's car.

"And that was really my first experience. Because it was totally different from my godmother's world and my world. Nice people would come to her house— people like John Wayne would come by. She was neighbor to the Bushes. She would take me to what's now the Galleria, and the salespeople would be there with clothes in their hands, and all I had to do was to point to what I wanted and I could take it home with me.

"And so I had never had a bad experience with people outside my race. I would hear about it, but it never happened to me. And I went through integration with the schools at that time. They had what you call 'bussing' back then, where you go over to the other side of town and try to blend in. And never had I experienced that [racism] in school. And with my godmother I never did.

I just couldn't believe that a grown man would go to a young lady and say that to me, and he didn't even know who I was.

Pointing to the white poster she carried in with her, I said "Can I ask about your poster?"

"Oh yeah—my poster is about Black History Month. And I guess because of that incident, I was more determined to keep up with Black History and bigotry and prejudice, so kids would be prepared for it. Because the kids around that time, the kids after me didn't know anything about that. They didn't get a chance to really live it. I don't want them to know about it *negatively*, but I do want them to know the *truth* that it does *exist*, even if it is hidden. Don't think it's just going to be a beautiful world all your life. It is not. So I go into all the schools and talk about Black History.

We returned to the subject of her experience in the entertainment business, and I asked, "Have you experienced anyone else being disrespectful of you?"

"No I have not. But that's not to say it's not happening to somebody else."

[She paused].

"But there is prejudice in the entertainment business. They wanted blacks to sing at white clubs. And after you got through singing, you had to *go*. But you couldn't sit on the same side with the white people. But you were good enough to come and perform for them, and after that you were cut off—no, nothing— like you never existed.

"But then when I grew up to be old enough to sell memorabilia for the different artists, I didn't see that, like it had faded away.

"But as far as changing in entertainment, I think Ed Sullivan did that. He was white, but he was maybe about the first to have black entertainment. We want the Jacksons! We want Diana Ross!

She laughed, thinking about these entertainers, but then she sighed and turned serious:

> "It was horrible. I mean it was like white people could just spit on you or hit you or hang you or beat you up, didn't have to be a reason. There's nothing to sugar coat it—it was horrible. But it was so long ago, it's not in mind anymore, but I would hear stories. Back then, I didn't really understand about Martin Luther King and the issues of what was going on, because I was in my little 'white world' with my godmother. So I didn't get a chance to see it in person."

One of the women who had accompanied her jumped in: "Explain your costume."

> "My costume? Oh. Okay—this side is like the 1800's when we were slaves, and cook and wear the aprons, and this side of me is like 'I'm every woman now.' So women of color started coloring and dying our hair like this [pointing] that's what that's all about and putting on makeup. That's why there's nothing on this side [makeup]. Because back in slavery times, there wasn't any makeup, and my hair is up in a bandana like it would have been during that time. You worked in the cotton patches. And if you were good, you'd be what you call the house 'N.' Back then, that was the main goal for a lot of people, to be in the house, instead of in the field in the cotton patches, in the heat. And so that's why I dress like this, for Black History, to let them know we have gone far."

This costume, then, was not a mark of mental illness as I had originally feared, but of creative pedagogy. She was using her costume to teach young people in her community about black history. What came across as eccentric was the boldness of someone who had grown up around the entertainment business and was not afraid to stand out. The poster she carried pictured her with the first black mayor of Houston, Lee Brown. She spoke of how she had been recognized for her efforts in organizing a festival for honoring Black History Month, and she had been given her own day.

Ms. Sherry Browning was a treasure. She had gifts to share. I felt embarrassed that I had originally found her strange. I did not directly ask about her costume, and instead it was brought up at the end of our conversation by one of the women accompanying her. Would it have been odd for me to ask about it sooner? I knew I didn't want to offend her or to make her feel that I found her outfit strange, but perhaps ignoring the outfit was a bit of an offense. Perhaps she wanted people to ask about it so she could share with them about Black History Month.

I am thankful for the story she shared with me. It showed how one racist encounter can stay with a person a lifetime. She hadn't spoken about that event in 40 years. And yet, she also had other experiences with white people that helped her remember: "Not all white people are bad." She was grateful for a particular relationship she had with her white godmother, and that relationship was what kept her from losing hope in all white people after her negative experience.

But this story is also about complex gratitude. When talking about her costume, she highlighted the enslaved women who worked in the master's house. She identified these people's jobs as the "main goal," being better off and more privileged than the men and women working in the fields. This phrase reminded me of her relationship with her wealthy white godmother. When people receive benefits from those in power, it can be harder to criticize the power structure.

White people who grew up with caregivers who were people of color serving as maids, nannies, or cooks often express that they experienced a mutual warm feeling of loving friendship. I think these experiences are real and genuine. Relationships of caring love can and do develop in such situations. But at the same time, such relationships are never equal. Persons in service positions do not have the freedom to show anything but loyal faithfulness for fear of losing their jobs. So while these feelings of love and care from household employees may be authentic, it is difficult to consider a different response coming from someone who benefits from being employed. Similarly, when Ms. Browning's white godmother lavished gifts of new clothes on her, I am sure her gratitude was real. But not having access to the same resources as the wealthy white woman, she may not have had a choice.

Ms. Browning's story also highlighted for me the importance of educating young people about black history. Black History Month is an important reminder of parts of our history we often overlook. While it has its limitations—some people argue that black history should be an integral part of a school's curriculum all year round instead of just one short month out of the year—it also serves a purpose in focusing on the work of black men and women who fought for their equal rights. Continuing with the theme of gratitude, honoring this history is an expression of gratitude for their work, a recognition of the contributions of black men and women who challenged unjust situations. Spending time learning about people who have overcome great adversity for the sake of equal rights for all, we express our gratitude for the ways they have taught us about what it means to advocate for oneself and on behalf of others.

In My Own Skin

I learned another lesson on gratitude in a conversation about race with a white student. This young man had been sent to see me by another professor, relating to the topic of his seminar paper. The student wanted to write about how white people have abandoned the heavenly kingdom in search of an earthly reward, while forcing black people and other non-white people to rely only on the heavenly reward. The other professor knew my work on race and suggested I could talk to this student about his paper subject, knowing it would be a sensitive topic. I had my concerns about the paper. I was worried about the student saying that all black people were religious as a way of dealing with oppression, since this is not true—there are plenty of people of color who have not been religious who have fought for justice out of a distinctly nonreligious perspective.[4]

But I also knew this student came from a different background than most of our students, and that he may need someone to think through this project with in an understanding way. I knew he came from a rural Texas town surrounded by poverty, having earned his undergraduate degree online. His residential seminary experience was the first time he had been in a community such as this. A man of deep faith, he was often seen as strange and not fitting in, and I knew he had said things in class that other students found offensive.

When we met in my office, I asked him to share with me the story behind this paper, since there were a lot of ideas in his paper that could turn into a much bigger project than this seminar assignment. He said that's what his other professor had told him, but that the other professor and I were "looking at the top of this large crap tree, seeing all these branches, when all I see is the root." I asked him what he saw as the root for this paper.

> "It started way back in the garden of Eden: the fig leaf. It's a symbol of division between man and man that just keeps on repeating throughout history. I know I've got to include a major section of an introduction just to say: 'Who am I to write this?' and to talk about myself as a white male and so on before I get to my topic. But the matter is that white people have focused only on finding their treasure here on earth, keeping it from everybody else, and it's the black people who are finding their treasure in heaven."

---

4   See Anthony B. Pinn, *When Colorblindness Isn't the Answer: Humanism and the Challenge of Race* (Durham, N.C.: Pitchstone Press, 2017). In this and in previous books, Pinn is critical of Christianity, saying it is unable to address the wrongs of racism that it helped institutionalize.

I told him my concern about talking about black people as all being religious, since that wasn't the case, and some people would feel offended by that. I asked whether he could talk about it just from the white perspective, writing to tell other white people about what he has learned from these readings and from class.

He said, "That's what the other professor said too. That I just need to write about it from the white side of things. But here's the thing. I don't identify with the white perspective. White culture, white privilege, white theology, I don't get any of it. But when I read black theology, that's when I really feel at home religiously. So I can't really write from that perspective, because that's not where I come from, and you're telling me I can't write from the black perspective because I'm white."

I responded, "So I hear you saying that class is also really important when considering religious perspectives." I was trying to understand him and build some common ground. "I know a few people have been writing on class, though not from a religious perspective." I pulled down a book from my shelf I had read in graduate school, entitled *A Place to Stand: Politics and Persuasion in a Working-Class Bar.* He looked at that book as I read the title and shook his head.

"But see? Right there, you're already above me. Those words, *working-class* and *bar* already are too high above the people I'm talking about, where I come from. People *I* know aren't even working-class, and don't have a bar to go to. They're too low to even make it into a class. It's what some people call 'white trash.' I'm talking about jail. I'm talking about jailhouse cultures and Appalachia and the 'trailer-hood'—where you can't even talk to anybody unless they're in prison, because that's the only place where you'll find them sober. Because once they're out, you won't be able to talk to them in their right mind again.

"Here, I may be able to walk into a white restaurant, or a white marketplace and get served, but back there I'm still just white trash. And I'm walking around and people know I'm white trash, and you get the door slammed in your face every time you try to ask for something. You have people walking around hopeless, who just don't care, who may never make a dollar in their life. And in a lot of ways they are worse off than oppressed blacks, the conditions they live in are worse off than many non-whites."

He paused before continuing. "And then you're telling them: you're not black, so you can't talk about black theology because you're white. But they've had white people their whole life telling them: 'No, no, no; you can't have that.' They see all this stuff that white people have, and they have none of it, so they don't see themselves as white. And I mean, white theology doesn't speak to them, and then you're saying they can't have black theology either. But I know the Bible, and that there's something in there about how *even the dogs get crumbs from the table.*"

He watched my reaction as he said this. "They've got to get something. And black theology is totally relevant to this culture."

My head was nodding and suddenly I was telling him, "That's your paper."

"I don't know if I could do that. You're asking me to crawl back into my own skin, crawl back into that hole. That's too painful. I don't know if I could do that. Because after this, I'm going home to that. I decided not to pursue ordination because I've seen things that make me think ministry is not about the gospel at all. So I don't know what I'm going to do, but I'm going to go back there, with those same people—and, I don't know, write? Am I going to write about this stuff? I don't know."

"You'd be offering us a real gift. You'd be writing about your experiences in that community, telling us about those people because they are not just 'those people'; they are people you know and love, people you care about—and people who are not hearing any good news from white theology and white religion. So *you* share with them the good news that you have found from reading these black theologians, and you write about what is the good news that you can bring back to that community."

"Okay. Okay. I think I got this. This is my paper, talking about my community, talking about black theology, then talking about white theology, and then talking about the good news for my community. I think I can do this. But man, this is going to be painful, to go crawling back into my own skin."

This student taught me about the power of gratitude. Even though he felt at first that he couldn't claim black theology for his community because he was white, this student experienced the liberating impact of black theology on his own life. He felt grateful for the ways that black theologians had helped him better understand the heart of God for the oppressed, an understanding that he had not heard from the white liberal theologians he was reading in his theology class. He felt black theology offered hope to his poor white community, a hope that he wanted to share with the people he knew from back home. He saw black theology speaking the good news of Jesus Christ to the poor whites of his hometown, and he was not going to let my concerns about his appropriation of their work get in the way of his connection to this material.

Acknowledging Class When Talking about Race

While working on my Ph.D. program at Emory, I took a philosophy seminar on theories of justice with a professor named

Liz Bounds. She was interested in my project, working on how white preachers can preach about racism to white congregations, so we met to talk at one point early in the semester. She asked me if I had come across any writings on class and race, because she was involved in a women's prison ministry that offered a certificate in theology to inmates. Many of the women she taught in that prison ministry were white. Talking about "white privilege" to a bunch of women locked away in jail, some of them facing death sentences, was not something that resonated with them. Liz Bounds wondered if I would be doing any economic social analysis in my work. She recommended the work of John Hartigan, a sociologist who has written about poor whites and their experiences.[5] I read some of his writings as I wrote my dissertation, but as someone who does not come from poverty, I had a hard time addressing issues of class directly. I wanted to be able to tell white people like me: we need to talk about race! I was more hesitant to say to white people like me: we need to talk about class.

Where I come from in Central Texas, success is measured in status and appearances. You have a good job? You look healthy and beautiful? Then you must be successful. And being successful also meant that you were blessed. Somehow, you being successful meant that God had looked upon you with favor, as if your success came about by your moral virtue. If you were not successful, if you were poor, or if you couldn't keep up appearances or lived in a poor neighborhood, then somehow you did not have the same favor in God's eyes. There was never any question of whether the system of wealth accumulation benefited some by discriminating against others, or if a person's success could be attributed to their inheritance of wealth. As a white person, I am barely able to understand white privilege. It is equally challenging for me to comprehend my class privilege as someone who grew up middle-class. It is much easier for me, and others like me, to believe even unconsciously that we are *morally* better than persons who are

---

5   John Hartigan, *Odd Tribes: Toward a Cultural Analysis of White People* (Durham, N.C.: Duke University Press, 2005).

poor, that we have had some special insight into how to succeed in life that others have been too lazy or stupid to learn.[6] But this belief is utterly *false.*

I know this is false just by looking at my own family. I come from a large family, in which I am the fifth daughter of six children; the youngest is a boy. School came easily for me, and I have been able to achieve goals in life that I have set my mind to accomplish—such as going to graduate school and becoming a professor. But what about the others?

My oldest two sisters have disabling mental illnesses. My sister Catherine, a star student growing up and a Texas state tennis champion, started showing signs of mental instability as a college student at Davidson. She has been in and out of hospitals over the years with schizophrenia, and because she is currently off her medications, she cannot take care of herself. She lives with my parents, who make sure she has food and drink set out for her to eat when she feels so inclined. But mostly, she lives on the couch, dirty for lack of bathing or ever changing her clothes. She will forcibly resist any attempts to groom her or to get her to the bathroom. She has the good fortune of a family who can take care of her and keep her safe and sheltered. But some people with schizophrenia are not so lucky.

I share this story about my sister because I always have in the back of my mind: *That could have been me.* It is by no power of moral fortitude or diligence on my part that I am able to care for myself and succeed in my career. It was a gift that I did not deserve or ask for, to be born with scholarly sensibilities and to not experience the mental illness of schizophrenia. Life is sometimes like that. It is not because God loves me more than my sister. It is a mystery.

And so I cannot attribute my own success to my own efforts, my own making. There may be truly "self-made" people out there,

---

6 For a great discussion of this tendency, see Tim Wise, *Under the Affluence: Shaming the Poor, Praising the Rich, and Sacrificing the Future of America* (San Francisco: City Lights Open Media, 2015).

but I do not know any. All of us who are successful have in some way been helped by forces outside our control. And in some cases, those forces were established legally to benefit some and not others.

The Myth of Meritocracy

There is a great three-part documentary entitled *Race: The Power of an Illusion.*[7] In the third segment, the history of housing discrimination gets played out across the 20th century, with the establishment of the GI Bill and the Federal Housing Authority. While black soldiers came home from fighting in World War II and had the same offer of a GI Bill to help them pay for a new home, very few of them were actually able to secure a mortgage due to discriminatory lending practices. Written into the original Federal Housing Authority mortgage underwriting was what was known as "redlining," showing which neighborhoods in a particular city were of "greater risk" than others. Those known as "greater risk" were the parts of town with a significant population of people of color and immigrants.

If a black soldier wanted to buy a home in what was a predominantly black neighborhood, he might be denied because his home would have been in an area deemed too risky to underwrite. If that same black solider wanted to buy a house in a predominantly white neighborhood—the areas in which he would be more likely to get a mortgage—he would be denied access because of discrimination (the house would be "no longer for sale" or "just gone off the market," a way for white neighborhoods to maintain racial segregation. So the black soldier and his family would have to rent their home, paying too high a rent for a home they could never own, spending money every month on rent that could have been building up equity for them in the form of home ownership.

---

7   Christine Herbes-Sommers, Tracy Heather Strain, and Llewellyn M. Smith, *Race: The Power of an Illusion,* directed by Christine Herbes-Sommers (California Newsreel, 2003), DVD or available on Vimeo. See newsreel.org.

A significant way wealth accumulates is through home ownership. As homes appreciate in value over time, the increase in value of the home will eventually be a source of income or inheritance to pass down to the next generation. But this is not always the case. If you are a person of color, your home may not appreciate in value if you are living in a less desirable (not white) part of town. So the rate of black wealth does not accumulate as fast as white wealth. If a black family moves into a white neighborhood, and then other whites decide to sell their homes and move to another neighborhood ("white flight"), then the increased number of homes on the market will decrease the value of the homes for sale. As more black families move into the neighborhood, the home values go down because of this same mentality: that these areas are not as valuable.

There is no such thing as a "meritocracy" in America. People who work hard and save their money can still end up at a great disadvantage from others simply because of the color of their skin. When we express our own gratitude for the gifts we have been given, we need to also be aware that our gratitude cannot be a denial of the history that led to the inequality we still see today.

Gratitude as a framework for talking about race and racism is not an easy idea. It is not an ignorance of inequality or injustice. Gratitude is the thankfulness we experience knowing God still loves us as we are, where we are, and yet calls us to act. Gratitude is not something we expect from others, but that we cultivate in ourselves to sustain us along the journey. Gratitude means accepting that God has given us gifts to share with others, knowing that our good intentions may be misinterpreted. Gratitude is a practice we work on and a gift we receive. We cannot expect ourselves to feel gratitude when we want to feel grateful, but we can try to cultivate gratitude within us and toward the God who aids us in feeling grateful.

Questions for Reflection and Discussion:

What makes you grateful? Do you think of gratitude as an appropriate response to discussions about race and racism? Why or why not? What benefits or disadvantages do you think could come from having a framework of gratitude when talking about these topics? Have there been times when you have experienced gratitude through discussions like this in the past? This chapter addresses a lot of sensitive subjects, such as white people's relationship with their caregivers who are people of color, and how our class background influences how we think and talk about race. What feelings did these topics bring up for you?

One of the sections mentioned the history of housing discrimination and its impact on wealth inequality. Thinking about your own housing situation, what kind of living situation did you experience growing up? What was the neighborhood like? Did your parents own their home or rent? If they owned their own home, did you see their home appreciate in value over the years? Did your parents' prosperity impact your own ability to own a home?

In thinking about patterns of discrimination that have resulted in segregated neighborhoods and schools, what are your thoughts about what might be a better solution? What kinds of efforts are you seeing in the area where you live to address these inequalities? Take time to write about these questions and then share them with another person. Remember to check in with your body to see where you are processing the emotions that come up in these discussions.

The Bible doesn't say anything about race. Let's leave it alone.

Chapter 6

SPIRITUAL PRACTICES FOR RACE TALK

You have read several chapters by now and you have learned about some stories that may be unfamiliar to you. You have shared with others about your own story and have heard about how others were brought up to think about race. You have hopefully had a chance to attend to your own emotional reactions during this time, letting yourself sit with them. But maybe this last part has been the most difficult. What does it mean to "sit with" our own emotions? And what does that have to do with faith?

As you continue long-term in the process of working against racial discrimination, I encourage you to consider practicing several spiritual practices. As a Christian, I grew up learning about traditional forms of spiritual practices, such as prayer and fasting. Some of the practices I discuss below may not sound as familiar to you from Christian history, but they can be found within the Christian tradition. These are the spiritual practices I want you to consider as you end your study of this book and respond to some of the concerns we have raised together: practices of caring for yourself through self-compassion, tending to cries for justice through bearing witness, strengthening community through hospitality and dialogue, and incorporating a vision of reconciliation in the regular forms of worship and preaching.

Self-Compassion

Self-compassion focuses on the second half of Jesus' commandment to *love your neighbor as yourself,* insisting that we cannot love our neighbor if we do not love ourselves. Self-care is often emphasized in seminary training, since pastors often spend many hours of the week caring for others—sometimes to the neglect of their own health. I tend to think of self-care as including making sure I get enough sleep and eat well, exercise from time to time, and make sure I spend time engaging in hobbies that renew my energy. But self-compassion is a little more intentional.

The spiritual practice of self-compassion is something that I borrow from reading the work of Dr. Kristin Neff.[1] Neff is a psychologist at the University of Texas who has written on self-compassion both for the scholarly community and broader public. Neff's understanding of self-compassion includes three things: mindfulness of one's suffering, a sense of common humanity, and an expression of loving kindness.

The first aspect of self-compassion, mindfulness of one's suffering, is simply a way of talking about how we need to acknowledge our difficult feelings. Neff emphasizes the importance of being mindful of our own suffering, because we have a tendency to ignore or deny these feelings. By giving ourselves a moment to focus our attention on these feelings, much like you have been doing in earlier exercises in this book, you are becoming mindful of your suffering, even if you do not particularly experience your feelings as "suffering." That's okay. The important thing is you are paying attention to them, whatever your feelings are in the moment. From having led many groups talking about race and

---

1   For a full list of her scholarship and books for the broader public, see Kristin Neff's website: self-compassion.org

racism, I can tell you a lot of feelings come up for me, and it is important to take a minute and tell myself: "I see you. I see what you're going through."

The second element of self-compassion is a sense of shared humanity, which means you allow yourself to acknowledge you are not the only one going through this experience in this moment. Suffering can leave us feeling very isolated. Believing we are the only ones going through a situation can prevent us from accepting our experience and building relationships with others. After participating in diversity workshops, I notice my tendency to want to be alone, to avoid being around other people. Not realizing the suffering we experience together in our shared humanity can prevent us from building connections with those around us.

The third part of self-compassion is loving kindness, the ability to offer yourself understanding and a nonjudgmental attitude. For many white people talking about racism, it is hard to avoid judging ourselves when we recognize racist thoughts or beliefs. We can judge ourselves and try to shut down our awareness of what is going on inside us. Acknowledging that others are also going through this assures us we are on a journey others are traveling also. That our complicity in racism gives us pain is a sign that our suffering is part of the process of growth. Knowing we have not "arrived" can allow us to be patient with ourselves, to encourage ourselves along this long journey. We can accept our feelings and failings and remind ourselves that God still loves us.

What does this look like in practice? When leading a workshop during a conference held at Montreat in North Carolina, I led the participants through a guided imagery prayer to help them cultivate self-compassion. You can use the following script to guide yourself or a group of others in a time of practicing self-compassion.

The prayer began by asking persons to sit comfortably and close their eyes, taking in deep breaths. (I encourage you to practice this as you read along.) After several moments of deep breaths, I invite each of them: "Imagine the healing balm of Jesus Christ, the Holy Spirit, being poured down upon your head, dripping down from the top of your scalp to your shoulders, down your arms, to your hips and down both legs. This healing balm of Christ, the Holy Spirit, is a word of grace being poured over you. In this moment, allow yourself to acknowledge that what you are going through right now is hard. This is difficult. What you are experiencing right now is a kind of suffering. Name to yourself the feelings that you are carrying in this moment.

"At the same time, there are others who are also going through this same thing. Others perhaps in this room are also suffering in the same way that you are. There are others around the world who share in this suffering to varying degrees. Feel yourself connected to them. And as you continue to take deep breaths, feeling yourself connected to all others who are suffering, imagine now the loving arms of your Savior Jesus Christ being opened to you, with the scars in his hands still visible. Imagine these loving arms wrapping around you, embraced by the love of a Savior who continues to be with you as you suffer, who sees what you are going through right now. Imagine those arms extending to surround persons suffering across your community, nation, and world. See Jesus' arms covering all who experience the kinds of suffering we have been discussing.

"And as you imagine these loving arms wrapped around you and the whole world, let yourself exhale with gratitude for the love God has shown to you. With every breath, let out an audible or inaudible, 'Thank you.' [I take an audible deep breath] 'Thank you.' [deep breath] 'Thank you.' You express your gratitude to God, to your loving Savior Jesus Christ, saying, 'Thank you.' You give thanks for the healing balm of the Holy Spirit, flowing down over you: 'Thank you.' You give thanks for the stories that have been shared with you, the individuals who have opened their hearts by sharing their experiences with you: 'Thank you.' You give thanks for the challenge of these kinds of conversations, the way they push us to think in new ways and to expand our network of concern, and call us to love our neighbor anew: 'Thank you.' We are thankful for the ways that our emotions respond to these stories and conversations, thankful that we can feel deeply: 'Thank you.' We give thanks for all of those who are working for racial justice, working to rebuild communities that remain divided; for these workers we say, 'Thank you.' We thank you, O God, for the ways that you work through us and in us, continuing to redeem us and calling us to share good news with the world. For all of this, we say, 'Thank you. Thank you.' [deep breath] 'Thank you.'"

At the end of the exercise, I invite the participants to remain in silence as they depart, carrying with them the thoughts and gratitude that they expressed through the guided prayer. I find this exercise helps many people attend to their emotions, to connect with God during a challenging time, and return to the world renewed with the confidence that God continues to work through them. This exercise helps me as well. I can feel my own anxiety lessen, my awareness of God's presence heighten, and my capacity to love myself and my neighbor deepen. Imagining Christ physically embracing us during the exercise helps us experience that love from God in a bodily way, beyond what we feel from simple verbal acknowledgment. We need to imagine ourselves physically embraced for our brains to send the message that we are indeed loved and cared for.

Bearing Witness

One of the other spiritual practices important for continuing the work of disarming racism is the practice of bearing witness. As with caring for the self, bearing witness also comes from the New Testament, specifically when Jesus instructs his disciples to go and be his witnesses to the ends of the earth. Self-compassion and bearing witness are as old as the commandments of Jesus.

To bear witness means several things. First, it means you are aware of the experiences of others, and you have close enough relationships to witness the things persons of color experience that whites do not. To witness something, you have to actually be there. And to be there, you have to be around people experiencing it. This means you need to consciously cultivate relationships with people different from yourself. If you live in a predominantly white neighborhood, it means intentionally making friends with the people on your block who do not look like everyone else. Get to know someone from a different country or background. Spend time with the families who have biracial children or transracial adoptees. Listen and learn from their experiences.

So the first thing about bearing witness requires proximity, being close enough to people who have experiences that are different from your own because of the color of their skin. This does *not* mean go and tell someone, "You can be my black friend!" But it does mean opening your eyes to the people of color you already come across in your life and finding ways to build relationships with them.

The second thing bearing witness means is you are *bearing* something. To learn about people's experiences involving racism or xenophobia, you are actually bearing their experiences with them. This doesn't mean you know exactly what they felt like when things happened, but it means in that moment you are recognizing the pain these experiences caused them, and you are not dismissing their experiences. To bear witness means to sincerely bear what they are telling you, not to suggest how their experiences could be reinterpreted. You are receiving them as they are told. You are honoring their sharing of these experiences with you.

And bearing also means you are feeling the impact on *you*. Pay attention to what feelings are being brought up in you. Intentionally bearing something means that we will feel its weight, and that can make us feel difficult feelings of our own. But to bear what has been shared, without becoming defensive or taking it personally, is to honor a moment of vulnerability and sharing.

Third, bearing witness means that you do not keep these incidents to yourself. When you see a black friend being pulled over by the police for no apparent reason, you serve as a real witness to this event, and you protest the action you see as unjust. You witness by telling others that racism is still a problem we need to be addressing across our society. You witness by trying to make a difference in your sphere of influence. Witness to the experiences of others, and share what you have witnessed with other groups of white people to say that racism is real, and by ignoring it we contribute to it.

What exactly are we witnessing to, besides painful experiences of discrimination against persons of color? There are other things we witness: we witness that society has changed, and yet still needs to transform. We witness the grace and power of God moving through groups of people who have been oppressed for generations. We witness the movement of God's Spirit calling on new leaders and generations of persons to take a stand on behalf of the most vulnerable. We witness the stirring of Christ's passion within us, calling us to become involved in some way. To all of these things, we are witnesses. To bear witness as a spiritual practice means to keep in mind these things while pursuing a life of justice. Taking time to give thanks to God for the many ways we can bear witness even now encourages us as we continue in our work.

Hospitality

Another spiritual practice we can engage in is hospitality. Hospitality can refer to a number of different actions—from the more concrete act of hosting someone in your home for a meal, to the more abstract act of welcoming another person into your heart. I think there is a rich spectrum of ways we can be hospitable toward one another.

In the sense of opening your heart to someone else, you are already doing that by reading this book. You are listening to the stories of others, people who may be different from yourself, and you are attending to their experiences. Such attention is a form of care. Even if it is only through reading this book, you are practicing a form of hospitality.

Being hospitable to someone else may also mean intentionally joining in conversations with persons you know to be on the other side of an issue. For instance, if you vote Republican, you may be practicing hospitality by having coffee with a friend who votes Democrat. Allowing space for the other person to share his or her thoughts, is another form of hospitality.

Talking about race is complicated. As mentioned before, race intersects a number of other ways individuals experience their identity. Persons who are both racialized the same can have very different experiences based on their economic status and other factors. Persons from the same family can have widely different experiences of race based on personal attributes. Sometimes, two siblings coming together to talk can be a sign of mutual hospitality if past conversations have been difficult. Conversations across differences of any kind can take place only because of a certain degree of hospitality.

Hosting dinners with persons from different groups may be an excellent way to intentionally build community in your city. Churches can connect across racial lines and build bridges through shared meals. Individuals can offer hospitality to others, opening their homes to make way for deeper communion. A group I have been part of in Austin called the Red Bench hosts monthly dinner gatherings for persons to come together and talk about difficult topics.

Churches have known for a long time that eating together is a powerful thing. The Lord's Supper, the last meal Jesus shared with his disciples, we commemorate in worship every time we share the Eucharist. Church potlucks may be as old as the first-century Christian communities. Sharing a meal is not something new to Christians, but making an intentional effort to share a meal with persons from a different community or perspective may be something out of the ordinary. Christians need to be able to build upon this familiar tradition of meal-sharing hospitality to build relationships with people who may be unfamiliar to them. Your church may already do something like this. Look into ways your church may already be hosting gatherings of people from diverse backgrounds under its roof or sponsoring such gatherings in other parts of your city or area.

Spiritual Practices of Worship and Preaching

This next set of practices may seem rather obvious: preaching and worship. You may be thinking, "Of course these are spiritual practices; why even talk about them?" I focus our attention on worship and preaching because these are the shared practices that the church engages in together on a weekly basis. This is where, together, you make up the body of Christ. And in worship we learn to listen for God's voice, to confess our sins before God, and to commit ourselves to living lives responsive to the grace that God has shown us. But what, exactly, does that have to do with the conversations about race and racism that we've been having?

That's a good question. You would not be alone in asking it. I was leading an afternoon workshop for a group of church leaders, both lay and clergy, who were sitting in a circle talking about the topic of diversity. Many people hear the word *diversity* and instantly interpret it as meaning "race." So I began by listing the many ways diversity is present in congregations: age, sexual orientation, gender, race, worship style, background, nationality, politics. I then asked the participants what they thought a preacher should say about diversity. If they were to look at this list and think of what they would want to hear a preacher preach about regarding any of them, what would that be? One person spoke up: "They shouldn't say anything. That's not what I came for. Sunday morning, I come to hear a sermon preached from the Bible, and none of those issues you've listed are in the Bible." *Are* issues of diversity present in the Bible? Specifically, what does the Bible say about *race*?

In some ways, it is anachronistic to suggest that biblical texts address race. Skin color as a category used to distinguish groups became systematized during the era of colonial expansion and the slave trade, at least a millennia after the latest writings in the Bible were penned. If white preachers relied only on the biblical text for guidance on what to preach about, they would never preach about race or racism, unless they chose to preach on the "slaves obey your masters" text, which most preachers typically avoid these days. The same could be said of other important issues that may not be named specifically in the Bible, and yet are topics preachers need to address in sermons. Additionally, avoiding preaching on race seems wrong when so much of the history of racism is connected to Christian practices of preaching.

Through much of the history of Christianity on the North American continent, Christians have largely been the source and proponents of racist ideology. When white Christians from Spain colonized the Americas, a racist understanding of humanity justified their treatment of indigenous people. When white Christians began baptizing enslaved Africans, they insisted that freedom in Christ did not make them free on earth. The history of the black church denominations in this country is one of segregation, through which white churches relegated black Christians to the balconies or did not allow them in at all. The Bible that we say is the word of God is the same Bible used by preachers to tell slaves to obey their masters. It is important that Christians respond to race *because of this history*. It is part of our heritage and we must address it. Worship and preaching provide us a great opportunity to engage these historical and lasting legacies.

Because racism is not just part of our history, but continues on today in the marches of white nationalists and more prevalent instances of discrimination and segregation, preachers and worship leaders need to name this sin in worship. Naming the problem of segregation and discrimination in our prayers of confession and prayers of the people can help remind us of our need to be mindful of the continuing struggle. Having in our church leadership persons that represent different groups of people also sends a message to all present that we are all made in God's image, so any of us can lift our voices in service to the praise of God. There are a lot of great resources for worship that recognize the diversity of God's beautiful creation, drawing from non-white authors of hymns, praise songs and prayers.

For preaching, there are a number of scriptural themes and texts that support and generate sermons on this topic. From the earliest dysfunctional family in the Bible, with Cain killing his brother Abel, we see the trajectory of humanity at war with itself. Noah's "curse of Ham," in which he curses his son Ham, was used to justify slavery.[2] A preacher can draw from these texts ways to inform the congregation of the history of racism and the harmful ways Christianity has fueled it.

A story about the leading figure of the Abrahamic traditions—how Abraham took his slave Hagar to have a child, and then abandoned her at the command of his wife Sarah—is, too, a story about slavery.[3] Biblical scholars have made connections between this text and the ways enslaved African women were forced to be concubines to their white masters and were also left to die, their children never recognized as part of the master's family.

The Exodus narrative of God bringing the Israelites out of slavery is a story that connects with many persons of African descent whose ancestors escaped slavery in the United States.[4] The Psalms and the voices of the prophets call out for justice on behalf of the oppressed; these too call our attention to the oppressed who are among us today. These are just of a few of the many passages just in the Old Testament that can foster rich discussions and sermons that address the history and ongoing legacy of racism

---

2 Stephen R. Haynes, *Noah's Curse: The Biblical Justification of American Slavery* (Oxford: Oxford University Press, 2002).

3 Delores S. Williams, *Sisters in the Wilderness: The Challenge of Womanist God-Talk* (Maryknoll, N.Y.: Orbis Books, 1993).

4 Eddie S. Glaude Jr. *Exodus! Religion, Race and Nation in Early Nineteenth Century Black America* (Chicago: University of Chicago Press, 2000).

and remind us that our brothers and sisters continue to suffer. The New Testament is also a rich resource for such preaching, and early Christian literature shows African theologians reflecting on difference from the beginning of the church's history.[5]

The framework for preaching on race I teach to my students includes the three processes of recognizing racism, recognizing ourselves within the story, and recognizing gratitude for the grace of God. Recognizing racism involves opening our eyes to the ways the scripture text informs our understanding of the subtle ways sin continues to operate in and around us, particularly through insidious and slippery expressions of racism. Recognizing ourselves within the story means that the preacher needs to help white Christians understand how racism impacts them, how they are connected to their brothers and sisters who continue to experience racism, and how their own spiritual growth is stunted through the system of racism. Recognizing ourselves includes understanding the difficult emotions that may be brought up for us as white people unaccustomed to talking about our whiteness. Finally, recognizing gratitude for the grace of God means looking within the text for the signs of God's grace that remind us God is already at work in us, continuing to work for our redemption. Gratitude is the third of these three processes because it is gratitude for God's grace that motivates us to live and act differently, not the shame of our sin. I encourage my students as they preach on difficult issues such as racism to look for a way to end with gratitude, some sign of the promises of God.

I helped to plan a church conference in North Carolina. The conference title was "DisGRace," and the focus was on finding God's grace amidst the disgrace of racism. Over the course of the event, we wanted to have three services of worship, and our planning team decided to pattern our worship on the three days of Triduum: Good Friday, Holy Saturday, and Easter Sunday. Prior to the event, a liturgical artist wrote lists of names on

---

5 Gay L. Byron, *Symbolic Blackness and Ethnic Difference in Early Christian Literature* (New York: Routledge, 2002).

long hanging banners that surrounded the sanctuary where we worshiped. The names were some of the many people of color whose lives have been lost because of hate and fear. Some of the names I recognized; many, I did not. At the end of the Good Friday service, members of the worshiping body brought down each banner and draped them onto the front table. It was a powerful statement, seeing the names of the dead laid out on the communion table, the place where we commemorate the sacrifice of Christ. We left the sanctuary in silence.

On the last day of the conference, we held a worship service that was themed with the message of Easter Sunday. As participants walked into the sanctuary, there in front—hanging high and brightly lit—were the names of the people; the banners that had been laid on the table, now lifted up. The message proclaimed that in our dying, we die with Christ. And as Christ lives and is raised from the dead, we too shall rise. This worship experience inspired me with hope that we can together mourn the injustice in our society, and we can pray for God's strength as we work. All those who have died as a result of injustice will not remain dead, but will rise with Christ, held forever by the love of the God who created each one by name. We *can* address these painful realities in our worship and preaching, and we must, to remind us all of the God who has called us together, to be one body.

Questions for Reflection and Discussion:

After reading, listening to the stories of others, and attending to your own emotions, what feelings do you have? My hope is that you feel a deep sense of gratitude for the people in your life who have shared their own stories with you. I hope you are feeling grateful for what they have contributed to your own understanding. I hope you feel gratitude toward the God who loves you even though your mistakes and sins are completely known. I hope you feel grateful for the love that calls you to new acts of love.

I also hope you feel an urgency that this is a subject we need to continue to talk about, because the repercussions of centuries of slavery and later forms of discrimination do not simply evaporate or age out. The legacy of racism is born anew and comes in new forms. I hope you are left feeling a sense of urgency to stay alert for the ways it re-emerges in your own context.

My hope is that, when you feel difficult feelings surrounding this topic, you will be able to notice what is going on inside of you and allow yourself those feelings without denying them or pushing them away.

I also hope you will share this book with people you know. Invite them to read it with you as you re-read it. Suggest that your small group at church or leadership team read it together. Or, find other books that talk about this subject in other ways. The goal is to stay aware and to continue to look for ways to engage with long-term efforts at racial justice.

If you are journaling while reading this book, I invite you to write down things you hope to do in the next year that keep you in this conversation. Is there a conference or an event you can attend? Is there an organization in your area you can join that's working on issues of justice with and for persons of color? Can you meet with the white people in your networks to talk about race? Can you put into practice some of the spiritual exercises talked about in this chapter? Can you work with people in your church to incorporate some of these ideas in worship? Take time to notice any experiences of gratitude you find along the way, and give thanks to God for the opportunities for new relationships.

But what I saw on the news...some people are crazy and racist. But that's not me. But how do I stop something like that happening in my town? I don't know. It makes me anxious.

Conclusion

THE ANXIOUS BENCH

The Second Great Awakening of the early part of the 19th century was a period of rapid growth of the Christian faith across the United States. Revivals happened in which thousands of people at a time would be saved. One of the most famous leaders of these revivals was Charles G. Finney, who wrote about the "New Measures," which he said were effectively leading people to Christ.[1] These New Measures included something called the "Anxious Bench." This was a seat—a long bench—positioned at the front of the sanctuary below the pulpit. This seat was reserved for persons who felt called to conversion. After the sermon, the preacher would call on the listeners to make a decision to commit or recommit themselves to God, and then the preacher would invite them to make that commitment public, coming forward to the anxious bench. Persons who felt so moved would rise from their seats and walk toward the pulpit, and sit at the Anxious Bench alongside others ready for conversion. Once seated, the preacher would then further exhort those on the bench to give their lives to God and to repent of their sins, dedicating themselves to godly living.

---

1 Ted A. Smith, *The New Measures: A Theological History of Democratic Practice* (Cambridge, United Kingdom: Cambridge University Press, 2007).

During these revivals of the 19th century, there was debate among religious leaders about whether or not these "New Measures" were actually helpful for leading individuals closer to God. A theologian and president of Marshall College, John Williamson Nevin, wrote a book in 1843 called *The Anxious Bench,* in which he criticized the practices of the New Measures, epitomized in his view by the Anxious Bench. Nevin believed that such practices actually distracted individuals from the movement of the Holy Spirit. Rather than focusing inwardly on the voice of God speaking to them in that moment, they were focused outward on needing to take this public action. Rather than having space to spend time with God in the quiet, they were made to interrupt any special illumination and instead give their time over to the anxiety of being in front of the entire assembly. Rather than being moved by God to make a decision, they were moved by their fear of what others would think and say, caught up in the pressure of the emotion of the moment. Such motivation, Nevin argued, would not produce a long-standing disciple of Christ, only persons who caved to external opinion.

I bring up this example of the Anxious Bench because talking about race can feel at times to be an "Anxious Bench" of sorts. It can seem that in order to show that you are a good white person, you need to be able to come before the assembly and admit that you are a sinner (someone with white privilege who is complicit in the larger system of white supremacy), and commit yourself to the work of anti-racism. To make such a profession is highly anxious, and it relies a great deal on the fear of others' opinion of you. Are you saying the right thing? Are you quoting the right people? Are you showing you have sufficient accountability from people of color? There are a number of ways white people can get overwhelmed with the imaginary list of qualifications to show they are "good white people."

So rather than making you, dear reader, commit to things you are not sure you entirely understand or believe, I want to give you the freedom to stay in your seat. You do not need to come forward to an Anxious Bench—either literal or figurative. I want you to be able to sit with your anxiety and not have to act out of it or because of it. I want any decision you make to commit yourself to the work of racial justice to come out of a thoughtful experience of learning from other people whose lives have been impacted by racism, and by white people who have experienced greater hope and community because of their work to further racial justice. I will not ask you to use the words "white privilege," though you may at some point recognize forms of white privilege you have previously been unaware of. I will also not insist you use the word "white supremacy" when referring to racism, though at some point you may see how naming white supremacy can be helpful to understanding what holds racism together over time. I will not ask that you make any public profession resembling a move toward an Anxious Bench, but I may suggest you sit with people who do not look like you next time you are in church or at a community event, so you can have a different experience of the world.

I do not want anxiety to be your motivation for changing your life. I want you to be motivated out of gratitude for the grace of God that is already at work in you.

I also recognize these are anxious times. Every few weeks more reports on the news tell us that racism is alive and well.[2] We may not identify with white people protesting the removal of Confederate monuments with openly racist speech, but their rhetoric and violence harms everyone in our society. Spending time learning about these events can make us anxious and fearful. Thinking of our friends and loved ones, we know persons of color who feel threatened by each reminder of white supremacy. The anxiety caused by the news requires that we pay attention to our reactions; listen to the feelings that emerge. Ask yourself:

---

2   Sheryl Gay Stolberg, "Hurt and Angry, Charlottesville Tries to Regroup from Violence," *The New York Times* (August 13, 2017). Accessed online at https://www.nytimes.com/2017/08/13/us/charlottesville-protests-white-nationalists.html

"Am I feeling numb? Angry? Helpless?" Pray for God's wisdom and courage to respond in solidarity. Respond not out of a sense of obligation to show your virtue to others, like appearing before the Anxious Bench. Respond out of the conviction that God is calling you to use whatever gifts you have to make a difference where you can.

Recommended Resources

Movies and Documentaries:

13th. Directed by Ava DuVerney. Performed by Melina Abdullah, Michelle Alexander, and Cory Booker. Kandoo Films, 2016. Documentary available on Netflix.

I Am Not Your Negro. Written by James Baldwin. Directed by Raoul Peck. Performed by Samuel Jackson and James Baldwin (archive footage). Velvet Film, 2016. DVD or available on Netflix.

Race: The Power of an Illusion. Episodes Produced by Christine Herbes-Sommers, Tracy Heather Strain, and Llewellyn M. Smith. California Newsreel, 2003. DVD or available on Vimeo. See newsreel.org.

Family Movies:

Hidden Figures. Directed by Theodore Melfi. Performed by Taraji P. Henson, Octavia Spencer, and Janelle Monáe. 20th Century Fox, 2017. DVD.

Home. Directed by Tim Johnson. Performed by Jim Parsons, Rihanna, Steve Martin, and Jennifer Lopez. DreamWorks Animation, 2015. DVD.

Zootopia. Directed by Jared Bush and Byron Howard. Performed by Ginnifer Goodwin, Jason Bateman, and Idris Elba. Walt Disney Pictures and Walt Disney Animation Studios, 2016. DVD.

Books:

Michelle Alexander, *The New Jim Crow: Mass Incarceration in the Age of Colorblindness* (New York: The New Press, 2012).

Beverly Daniel Tatum, *"Why Are All the Black Kids Sitting Together in the Cafeteria?" And Other Conversations about Race* (New York: Basic Books, 1997).